THE GLUTEN-FREE
ITALIAN
COOKBOOK

The Wheat-Free Gourmet

THE GLUTEN FREE

ITALIAN

COOKBOOK

*Classic Cuisine
from the Italian
Countryside*

MARY CAPONE

The Gluten-Free Italian Cookbook: Classic Cuisine
from the Italian Countryside is published by The
Wheat-Free Gourmet Press, a division of The Wheat-
Free Gourmet™, 5836 Park Lane Road, Longmont,
CO 80503.

E-mail: wfg@wheatfreegourmet.com

Websites:
www.wheatfreegourmet.com
www.bellaglutenfree.com

Cover and text design by Jill Hadley

Library of Congress Cataloging-in-Publication Data
available upon request.

ISBN 978-0-615-21909-7

Printed in the United States of America

First Printing: October, 2008
Second Printing: July, 2010
Third Printing: April, 2011

Acknowledgments

—◆—

I dedicate this book to my kitchen angels, all the beautiful relatives who have gone before me and continue to whisper their culinary magic in my ear. My father Anthony Capone, Aunt Carmel Adnolfi, Uncle "Zio" Joe D'Giavonniantonio, Nonna Angelina Capone, Nonno Tuffy Levo, Great Grandmother Angeline Levo and my brother Mark Capone. You hold a special place in my memory, full of recipes, stories, food and love.

I thank my mother Angeline, my sisters Camille, Marcia, and Angela and brother Gerard for their incredible enthusiasm and encouragement throughout this project. You never let me forget this book was needed, nor that I could do it. You guys are the greatest.

To Jill Hadley, my designer and editor, without whom this book would still be in scraps of paper, piles of recipes, dirty plates, and mental notes, I thank you. Your dedication to the project and the beauty you bring to it has been a great inspiration for me.

To my students of *The Wheat Free Gourmet Cooking School*, my army of recipe provers, thank you for always showed up so willing to create together. Your feedback and your company is highly regarded.

To my husband, Tim Benko, for his beautiful photography throughout the book. I am always amazed at how he can transform a photograph into a living thing. My food never looked better.

Finally, a special thanks to my two daughters, Maya and Raven, who have listened to me talk about food non-stop for years, and who have eaten more than their share of test recipes. And even though some days they cry wolf, "I can't possible eat another thing, Mom," or "I just can't talk about food right now, OK," the next day they are fresh and ready to listen and taste again. I love you more than food itself, and that's saying a lot. This book is for you.

Contents

———◆———

Aunt Carmel and her daughter, Cathy. Opposite page: Dad

Introduction

*I*talians have a saying, *"Mangiare bene, bere bene e' vivere bene."* To eat well, to drink well is to live well. That's how I like to live my life, spending hours creating in my kitchen, filling long tables with delicious platters of food, surrounded by loved ones and laughter.

My paternal grandfather was the wine maker of our "Little Italy" in upstate New York. By all rights this book could have been about wines if that were the knowledge I had pursued, but it was the kitchens that drew me in. My Aunt Carmel's shiny stainless steel stove, lined with bubbling pots, lured me with its secret scent-filled symphony. The enticing aromas of braised meats in tomato sauce wafted from my grandfather's window as I played jacks with my cousins in his stone courtyard. The acre-long city garden of my Uncle Zio Joe was my edible playground, its bounty filling the folds of my skirt as I followed him down narrow, earthy paths.

And there was my father's kitchen. I'd sit on my high stool and stir a pot of minasta or grate a hard chunk of Parmesan cheese over a steamy bowl of pasta. We'd have long talks, as he prepared the mid-day meal, about school and friends but mostly about the glories of the food we were eating. And when words ran out, my father would hum a soft tune, filling his food with melodic cadence. My childhood memories are intertwined with the scrumptious smells of garlic and fresh tomatoes, gentle conversations and laughter. I come by my love of food naturally, for in each of these kitchens, food was an expression of love and love was in the food.

After college, I left home and traveled to Europe where I found a passion for the culinary arts that matched mine. I spent a year traveling through southern Europe. When I crossed the Italian border, I felt a deep sense of home. The language sang to me. The faces were so familiar that any one of them could have been my relative. But it was the food that connected my Italian-American heritage to this beautiful culture. I finally understood that my need for artistry, my passion for great food, my never-ending quest to raise the palate, came from the mother country, Italia.

While in Italy, I returned to my father's family village and became an instant celebrity. I was the first cousin to have returned since World War II. There I learned the secrets of simple southern Italian cuisine. I can still see my cousin Maria picking produce from her garden for our dinner and Pasquale and his wife preparing a freshly slaughtered pig for the special occasion. My cousin Angelina's singsong voice calling me from my afternoon siesta lives in my memory, as does her giant bowl of caffè latte, and bean and tomato soup.

I spent most of that year in Italy, traveling from north to south, studying wonderful classic cuisines. It was the dishes from my grandmother's village that captivated me the most.

When I returned to the States, I was so inspired by the cuisine of Europe that I started *Marie's Crepes,* a European-style kiosk that offered crepes made to order. About this time, I began to notice that my health was faltering. I started presenting signs of a serious autoimmune disease, one that had eventually caused the death of my grandmother. From that point on, I bore many years of misdiagnosis from doctors who told me it was genetic, and that there was nothing I could do about it. Finally, as many of us have come to, I diagnosed myself and then later had it confirmed by a gastro-intestinal doctor that I had celiac disease. What a blessing — immediately after removing gluten from my diet, I began to regain my health in good stride.

But how could I continue to indulge my passion for Italian food? When I finally understood that the lovely, yet gluten-rich diet of my ancestors was the problem, I turned to food for the cure. Instead of concentrating on what it was that I could not eat, I began a culinary journey with the quest of discovering just how many delicious foods I could reshape and create new. I started in my home kitchen with old family recipes, converting them one by one into healthful, gluten-free alternatives. I pursued gluten-free food with the same passion as I had the more traditional cuisine, determined to make my creations more enticing than the original recipes. My desire was, and still is, to invite the gluten-free palate to sing with flavor.

In 2005 when my recipe books were full, I started *The Wheat-Free Gourmet Cooking School* in Boulder, Colorado, one of the first gluten-free cooking schools in the country. Here I found a lovely community of students, all coming to together with stories and information. The school's kitchen was always a buzz of excitement, joy and laughter as we explored and proved together recipe after recipe. I can honestly say I have never met a celiac I didn't like. There is something about the grassroots celiac community we have created in this country that has kept us full of compassionate understanding for each other.

It is in this spirit of love that I decided to write this cookbook for gluten-free dieters, sharing with you the recipes and stories of my youth. This book is inspired by my beautiful relatives who have gone before me, and by their lives that were filled with home-cooked food and kitchen stories. This book is an invitation for you to return to the pure joy of cooking and to the delirious love of food again.

In the tradition of all that have gone before me, I raise my glass to you.

Cento Anni.

I hope you live a hundred years.

Mom, Uncle Albert, Uncle Bobbie and Uncle Tony
Opposite page: Grandmother and Grandfather Capone

The Gluten-Free Palate

*T*he cuisine of Italy is filled with fresh ingredients; vine ripened vegetables, grains and proteins combined in a way that is inherently healthy. But like everyone else, in food it is the tantalizing aromas and vibrant flavors that I seek. When I bring a forkful of lasagna to my mouth, I anticipate several layers of flavor to ignite my palate; the tangy sweet burst of sun-ripened tomatoes, the rich creamy filling, the Parmesan cheese pasta wrapping the flavors in a bit of textural heaven. Essentially, I expect my mouth to sing with flavor.

The gluten-free palate should accept nothing less. Many people get confused when first entering the "forbidden world" of the gluten-free diet, concentrating on the foods that they can't eat and forgetting about the world of foods they can. They become momentarily paralyzed, like deer in the headlights, avoiding everything they imagine has been touched by flour-laden hands. Then, they begin to move. Gathering their courage, they march into the commercial markets, scouring aisles, reading tiny labels until they're blurry-eyed. And although they might find a few good choices, commercial foods will never quite fill the void that resides deep in their bellies for a savory home-cooked meal. If anything, the pining for these sensuous foods grows louder. What is the solution? A return to the home kitchen. With the right recipes, a new look at flours and how to combine them and a chef's imagination, you can create beautiful gluten-free cuisine that rises far above the foods you ate before. Foods that will engage your palate, excite your senses and feed your body well. Classic cuisine that will make your mouth sing. Now won't your friends be jealous?

The science of gluten-free flours

The biggest complaints I hear from my students are their disastrous experiments with gluten-free flours. I commiserate and tell them to try to forget the wheat flour-based baking they once knew, for it is a brave new baking world. Accept that a scoop of white rice flour will act nothing like a scoop of wheat flour. Here's why:

Gluten is a storage protein found in wheat, rye and barley. When you add liquid to wheat flour with an action such as kneading or mixing, you create the stretchy quality that bakers love. In bakers' terms, gluten is the "glue" that holds the dough together, giving it its elastic properties, texture and structure. Heat assists in developing this texture; cold retards it.

Gluten-free flours, however, are more challenging. They do not have the ability to develop this elasticity, even with heat, kneading or mixing. Besides, most good gluten-free dough is very sticky and does not lend itself to kneading by hand. Rather, the gluten-free baker needs to learn new techniques and formulas. Ingredients like xanthan gum, guar gum, eggs and egg whites, and leavening agents will help create elasticity. Different flours and starches such as potato starch, tapioca flour and sweet rice flour will aid in developing structure. Techniques such as using warm liquids and eggs, as well as beating and ribboning, will add air to batter and give lightness to the final creation. These techniques are discussed in detail throughout the book.

Essential to successful gluten-free baking is a good baking mix. I hardly ever use gluten-free flours individually; they work best in combination. I have created two flour combinations: Mary's Baking Mix is designed for use in pastas, breads and crepes — dishes that don't require extra "puffiness". Mary's Baking Mix II is used in fine pastry dough, cakes and cookies that require extra structure and moistness.

For my baking mix, I use a simple combination of white and brown rice flour, potato starch and tapioca flour. Rice flour is the base, and a combination of brown and white lightens the texture of baked goods. If you want a more nutritious mix with a lower glycemic index (lower indexes mean food takes longer to turn into blood sugar), use all brown for the rice flour component.

I encourage you to keep a batch of Mary's Baking Mix on hand. Most of the recipes in this book are written with this mix in mind. It is so much easier to have the mix prepared — then you can just scoop and go.

I like to use Mary's Baking Mix II for pastry baking. I have added sweet rice flour, or mochi, to the mix. Sweet rice flour is a thickening agent, and it also gives baked goods more texture and helps keep them moist.

Also, either mix can be substituted for the other without notable difference. If you don't have the specified mix on hand, don't hesitate to use the other. Either one will give you good results.

MARY'S BAKING MIX

MIX IT UP

❧ Blend flours well with whisk and use.

❧ Refrigerate any unused portion in a tightly sealed container. Mary's Baking Mix can stay fresh in the refrigerator for up to 4 months.

Ingredients

2 cups brown rice flour

2 cups white rice flour

1⅓ cups potato starch

⅔ cup tapioca flour

MARY'S BAKING MIX II

MIX IT UP

❧ Blend flours well with whisk and use.

❧ Refrigerate any unused portion in a tightly sealed container. Mary's Baking Mix II can stay fresh in the refrigerator for up to 4 months.

Ingredients

2 cups brown rice flour

2 cups white rice flour

1⅓ cups potato starch

⅔ cup sweet rice flour

A word about gluten-free flours and starches

Here is some basic information about each of the gluten-free flours and starches that I like to use in baking, as well as some that I am still experimenting with. I don't wander far from Mary's Baking Mix or Mary's Baking Mix II since using them has resulted in light and fluffy baked goods; well-textured breads, pizzas and pie crusts; and elastic crepes. These mixes make a great foundation for the addition of other flours and starches. Feel free to keep experimenting until you find your signature mixture.

Amaranth is easily digestible flour that is high in fiber, iron and calcium. When combined with brown rice flour, it results in a complete protein as high in food value as fish, poultry or red meat. When combining it with other flours, add one part amaranth to 3–4 parts other flours. It can be used by itself to make flatbreads, pancakes and some biscuits.

Arrowroot is nutritious flour that is very fine and easy to digest. It is used primarily to thicken sauces in place of a *roux*. Arrowroot is similar to cornstarch, and they can be exchanged measure for measure. It doesn't require high heat to thicken, has very little taste and gives sauces and stews a glossy finish. I actually prefer it to cornstarch.

Chickpea flour, made from garbanzo beans, is high in protein and nutrition. The late great Bette Hagman used it as a primary component in her baking mixes. It has a slightly heavier taste and is best used in baking bread.

Brown rice flour is one of the most common flours used in gluten-free baking and cooking. More nutritious than white rice, it is milled from unpolished brown rice and contains bran. It has a low to medium glycemic index of 57. The oil in the bran makes it more perishable, and it needs to be refrigerated to keep the taste fresh. Since it is a primary component in my baking mixes, the mixes should be kept refrigerated as well.

Corn flour is made from milled corn and can be used in corn bread, pancakes and muffins.

Cornmeal is ground white or yellow corn with a gritty consistency. This is the flour I use to make polenta. Bob's Red Mill offers a yellow cornmeal that is guaranteed gluten-free, and I also use a gluten-free Italian import of *Sala Cereali,* a finely ground cornmeal flour that cooks in 5 minutes, which you can order online.

I avoid U.S. corn products because they have been exposed to genetically engineered organisms, or GMOs. GMOs create new foods that have built in anti-nutrients that humans have never before been exposed to. With natural cross-pollination through the air of corn, many believe that most of the corn across America has been contaminated by GMO corn.

Cornstarch is a refined starch derived from corn. It is used to thicken sauces and add silkiness to a baking mix. If you are allergic to corn, substitute arrowroot in equal amounts.

Guar gum is a natural food thickener similar to locust bean gum, cornstarch and tapioca flour, and it is often used as a additive in puddings and ice cream. Guar gum is also used as a binder similar to xanthan gum, although you would use far less for similar results. I do not

use guar gum in baking, since in large amounts it can cause stomach distress, but many gluten-free bakers swear by the combination of xanthan and guar gum.

Nut flours such as almond, walnut, hazelnut and chestnut are high in protein and therefore will increase the nutritional value of your food. Although they can be bought at the health food store, they are quite expensive and can be made easily in a food processor or a coffee grinder reserved for that purpose only. Add 1 tsp sugar to prevent the nuts from turning into butter, and pulse or grind only until you have fine meal quality, about 1 minute. Gluten-free chestnut flour can easily be found on the web. There are several companies that import this flour from Italy. I like to use chestnut flour for pasta, breads, and even a nutty pancake.

Potato starch is derived from potatoes and is fine white flour that I use in Mary's Baking Mixes. Do not confuse it with potato flour, which is much denser and heavier in taste. Potato starch adds silkiness and structure to bake goods. If you are allergic to potatoes, you can substitute cornstarch in equal amounts.

Quinoa flour is an ancient grain that is actually derived from a fruit. It is a superfood loaded with protein (touted as being the highest source of protein from a fruit source), and it is also high in phosphorus, iron, calcium, vitamins B and E and fiber.

Sorghum flour is bland, light-colored flour that is relatively new to the United States, although it has been a primary source of nutrition in Africa and India for centuries. Due to its protein and starch configurations, it digests slowly and may be especially healthful for diabetics. High in iron, potassium and calcium, it also has anti-cancer properties. It may be used as a substitution for brown rice flour in small amounts. It is also called milo, jowar or cholam flour.

Soy flour is high in protein and has a distinctively nutty taste. It combines well with other flours and can be used for breading or baking. Store in the refrigerator or freezer, for it has a short shelf life.

Sweet rice flour, or mochi, is flour made from glutinous (but still gluten-free) rice. Its sticky properties make it an excellent thickening agent for sauces, pie crusts and breads. It enhances the structure of baked goods and even helps to keep them moist. Asian shops and health food stores will have this flour but they may call it mochi.

Tapioca flour and **tapioca starch** are virtually the same in properties and can be used interchangeably. Also named cassava or manioc flour, it combines well with other flours such as brown rice and potato starch and helps create structural integrity and elasticity in baked goods. I also like this flour for dusting meats and vegetables for frying and often create a tapioca *roux* for gravies and sauces. Tapioca flour can be stored at room temperature and has long shelf life.

Xanthan gum is not a flour but an essential component to any successful gluten-free baking mix. It is, in fact, a friendly bacteria that comes from corn sugar and acts like the "glue" in gluten-free foods. Without it, our gluten-free breads and baked goods would lack texture, elasticity and sponginess and would simply crumble in our hands. Guar gum can be used as a replacement or in combination with xanthan gum although it may act as a laxative for some.

Safe and Forbidden Grains

SAFE FOODS AND GLUTEN-FREE GRAINS:

Amaranth, arrowroot, bean flours, buckwheat, chickpeas, corn, garfava, Job's tears, mesquite (pinole), millet, montina (Indian ricegrass), potato, quinoa, ragi, rice, sorghum, tapioca, taro root, teff and coconut flour.

According to the latest research, these foods have cleared the questionable list: Alcohol (distilled). caramel color, citric acid, dextrin, flavoring extracts, vinegar (except malt vinegar), wheat grass and yeast (except brewer's yeast).

FORBIDDEN GRAINS:

Wheat, barley, rye, triticale (hybrid of wheat and rye) and oats (except for ones marked gluten-free).

Here are some other names of grains that contain gluten and should be avoided: Bulgur, cake flour, couscous, durum, einfkorn, flour, frumento, graham, kamut, matzo, matzah, seitan, semolina, and spelt, which is often marketed as a wheat alternative but it is loaded with gluten.

Measurement Equivalents

DRY INGREDIENTS		LIQUID INGREDIENTS	
1 TBL	3 tsp	8 oz.	1 cup
1 cup	16 TBL	2 cups or 16 oz.	1 pint
3/4 cup	12 TBL	4 cups or 32 oz.	1 quart
1/2 cup	8 TBL	4 quarts or 128 oz.	1 gallon
1/3 cup	5 1/3 TBL		
1/4 cup	4 TBL		
1/8 cup	2 TBL		
6 oz. chocolate	1 cup chocolate chips		
1 stick butter	4 oz. or 1/2 cup		

Substitutions

1 cup brown sugar (packed)	=	1 cup granulated sugar
1 cup milk	=	1 cup milk alternative such as gluten-free almond, soy, rice, hazelnut or coconut milk
1 tsp baking powder	=	1/4 tsp baking soda plus 1/2 tsp cream of tartar
1 cup oil	=	1 cup butter, ghee or butter alternative
1 TBL fresh herbs	=	1 tsp dry herbs

potato starch can be exchanged for equal amounts cornstarch

tapioca flour can be exchanged for equal amounts sweet rice flour

brown rice flour can be exchanged for equal amounts white rice flour

1 ounce unsweetened chocolate can be exchanged for 3 TBL unsweetened cocoa powder and 1 TBL vegetable oil

A Gluten-Free Kitchen

A key to maintaining a gluten-free kitchen is to have the right tools on hand. With a foolproof recipe, a container of Mary's Baking Mix, a well stocked gluten-free kitchen pantry and the right kitchen equipment, you are ready to become a great gluten-free chef.

The list of ingredients I have included is based on the recipes in this book. This list will also serve as a good base for any gluten-free pantry. Feel free to add more of your favorite ingredients. Just make sure to check the labels and/or call the manufacturer about their products and facilities.

How to use this book

All the recipes have been carefully scrutinized and eaten by me and a host of students of *The Wheat-Free Gourmet Cooking School.* Still, if there are some ingredients that are questionable for you, don't use them. Chances are you already know any additional foods that don't make you feel well. So when it doubt, leave it out, and substitute a food your body does well with. You are the chef in charge of your kitchen. The final decision is yours.

Throughout the book, I have offered dairy-free, casein-free recipe variations. All but a few recipes are soy-free and corn-free. Enjoy all that this book has to offer. There are many great choices for dishes that can feed your desire for delicious food as well as help you heal.

Avoiding cross-contamination

If you live with *WE* people (wheat eaters), here are a few simple tips on how to avoid cross-contamination. Reserve an airtight container for your baking mix. (In my kitchen, I draw the line at wheat flour and don't allow it at all.) Claim a refrigerator shelf and gluten-free space in your cupboards for your gluten-free flours and other ingredients. Make separate cutting boards gluten-free space, and use a separate sponge or cleaning brush when washing appliances, surfaces or dishes. A dishwasher is good tool to sterilize plates and mixing bowls. Buying a separate toaster reserved for gluten-free eaters will save you from the crumb wars.

Introducing Bella Gluten-Free

No time to make the Mary's Baking Mix? You can substitute Bella Gluten-Free All Purpose Mix, an allergen-free dry mix designed by Mary for recipes using her Baking Mix I or II. You simply add the called for amount of baking mix and eliminate the salt and xanthan gum. (If the recipe calls for more than 1 tsp of xanthan gum, add the recipe amount minus 1 tsp). Order Bella Gluten-Free All Purpose Mix and other fine dry mixes at www.bellaglutenfree.com.

Ingredients for the Pantry and Refrigerator

- **Bella Gluten-Free Dry Mixes:** 100% natural allergen-free dry mixes designed by author Mary Capone, available at www.bellaglutenfree.com
- **gluten-free broths** (Pacific Foods has a great selection of organic gluten-free broths)
- **gluten-free baking soda**
- **gluten-free baking powder**
- **chocolate:** milk, bittersweet, gluten-free chocolate chips, dark chocolate
- **dry unsweetened cocoa**
- **cooking spray**
- **cornmeal** or polenta
- **chickpea flour** or garbanzo bean flour (refrigerate after opening since it is not used often)
- **chestnut flour** (refrigerate after opening since it is not used often)
- **large eggs** (I like to use cage-free organic eggs when I can)
- **egg replacer** (for egg replacement made by Ener-G Foods, see ener-g.com)
- **herbs:** fresh when possible, such as Italian flat-leaf parsley, oregano, sage, thyme, rosemary, marjoram
- **almonds, walnuts and pine nuts,** raw and unsalted (refrigerate all nuts)
- **oils:** olive oil, coconut oil, grape seed oil and canola oil
- **gluten-free pasta** (when there is not time to make fresh pasta, I like Tinkyada, Pasta of Joy)
- **potato starch**
- **rice flours:** white rice flour, brown rice flour and sweet rice flour or mochi (refrigerate brown rice flour)
- **sea salt,** coarse and fine
- **spices:** cinnamon, nutmeg, red pepper flakes, white pepper, black pepper
- **Bragg's Liquid Aminos** (this is a non-fermented soy sauce that is gluten-free)
- **sugars:** granulated sugar, light and dark brown sugar, powdered sugar
- **tapioca flour** or tapioca starch
- **Thai Kitchen condiments** (all of their sauces such as Sweet Red Sauce and Spicy Thai Chili are gluten-free)
- **extracts:** gluten-free vanilla, almond, hazelnut, lemon, orange, lavender, cherry, strawberry, rose (I buy unusual flavors at faeriesfinest.com)
- **balsamic vinegar**
- **xanthan gum**

Equipment List

There are a few pieces of equipment that are very helpful in the making of a successful gluten-free kitchen. Since gluten-free batter and dough are often stickier than traditional wheat dough, I rely on machines to do the mixing. For pastries, cakes and fillings, I use a heavy hand mixer. For breads, I use either a food processor or heavy hand mixer. And, of course, there is the pasta machine. Either a traditional hand-crank or an electric version will do the job well. My favorite is the pasta roller attachment to the Kitchen Aid®.

MACHINES

- **heavy hand mixer** such as a Kitchen Aid or a stand mixer (you can start with a hand mixer, but add a heavy hand mixer to your wish list)
- **food processor:** 9–11 cup capacity for breads, or 6–7 cup capacity for most other recipes
- **blender**
- **coffee grinder** used specifically for nut flours

ASSORTED GADGETS

- mixing bowls: glass or plastic, assorted sizes
- measuring cups and measuring spoons for dry ingredients
- glass liquid measuring cups
- wooden spoons
- slotted spoon
- cooking tongs
- chef's knife, 8" or 9"
- paring knives
- serrated bread knife
- spice and fruit zester
- pastry bags and nozzles: #10 and #16
- parchment paper
- rubber spatulas
- kitchen timer
- oven thermometer
- cake thermometer
- assorted whisks
- mortar and pestle for herbs and spices
- rolling pin
- cooling racks

The Wheat-Free Gourmet Cooking School

STOVE AND BAKING PANS

- medium and large heavy-bottom skillets
- 6-quart Dutch oven
- double boiler
- small, medium and large saucepans
- stock pot for pasta and soups
- 9–10" crepe pan
- 9–11" springform pans (they are often sold in threes and are quite reasonable)
- 9" tart pans
- 9" glass or ceramic pie pans
- 2–4 baking sheets or heavy-duty cookie sheets
- 6 ceramic ramekins
- 12-cup muffin tin or two 6-cup muffin tins
- 9x13" or similar size baking dish, glass or ceramic

Author Mary Capone, The Wheat-Free Gourmet

Other important ingredients

Sea salt. Throughout this cookbook I recommend adding sea salt to the recipes. An unrefined sea salt (not processed) literally feeds the body important minerals such as calcium, magnesium, sulfates and other trace minerals that iodized table salt does not. Iodized table salt is mainly sodium chloride and not salt at all. Salt, an essential flavor enhancer, is also critical in the baking process, especially with yeast breads. I suggest finely grated sea salt, which you can find at a health food store.

"Good" oils. A famous naturopathic doctor explained the most important foods that we put in our bodies are, in this order: good oils, proteins, fruits and vegetables and carbohydrates. But what are "good" oils? We hear a lot about the benefits of canola oil, and next day we hear that it is bad for you. Writing an Italian cookbook made it easy for me to choose cold-pressed, extra virgin olive oil as my main component. Since I do very little high heat frying, the oil will not loose its nutritional value. I also use pure butter in baking, and recommend ghee or palm oil as an excellent alternative for dairy-free, casein-free eaters. Here is my list of good oils:

Olive oil. High in antioxidants and monounsaturated fatty acids, olive oil has been shown to offer protection against heart disease by controlling LDL ("bad") cholesterol levels while raising HDL ("good") cholesterol levels. No other naturally produced oil has as large an amount of monounsaturated fatty acids as olive oil. Olive oil is very well tolerated by the stomach, and its protective function has a beneficial effect on ulcers and gastritis. When buying olive oil, you will want to obtain high quality extra virgin oil. The oil that comes from the first "pressing" of the olive is extracted without using heat (a cold press) or chemicals. The less the olive oil is handled, the closer to its natural state, the better the oil.

Coconut oil. Coconut oil is edible oil that has been consumed in the tropics for thousands of years. Studies done on native diets high in coconut consumption show that these populations are generally in good health and don't suffer as much from many of the modern diseases of Western nations. With a long shelf life and a melting point of 76 degrees, I like to use this oil for high temperature frying. The nutty, slightly sweet taste adds another flavor element to a dish.

Grape seed oil. Grape seed oil's healthful qualities have been appreciated for over 100 years. Also called grape oil, it has become a kitchen favorite because of its clean, neutral taste and high heat cooking ability.

Butter. Butter is my favorite fat for baking. Although it is a dairy product, it contains only traces of lactose, so moderate consumption of butter is not a problem for the lactose intolerant. People with casein allergies, however, need to avoid butter, which contains enough of the allergy-causing proteins to cause reactions. Throughout the book I have offered suggestions for butter alternatives.

Ghee is a class of clarified butter made by simmering unsalted butter in a large pot until all water has boiled off and the milk protein has settled to the bottom. The cooked and clarified butter is then spooned off to avoid disturbing the milk solids on the bottom of the pan. Ayurvedic texts say that ghee helps balance excess stomach acid and helps maintain and repair the mucus lining of the stomach. Ghee also has a very high smoke point and is ideal for high heat cooking

Earth Balance Buttery Sticks®. This is a good trans fat-free margarine. It is vegan vegetable shortening that is that is made without hydrogenation, trans fatty acids and dietary cholesterol. It is also dairy and egg-free, with nothing artificial added. It does contain some soy. I like this as a butter alternative for baked goods in particular.

Palm oil in shortening form is a healthy, trans-fat free alternative to traditional shortening for baking. It's packed with nutrients and provides a valuable source of beta carotene and vitamin E. Studies have found that tocopherols and tocotrienols, which are isomers of vitamin E found in palm oil, are antioxidants and may be associated with more favorable cholesterol profiles, and lower risk of heart disease. If you are allergic to or are avoiding soy, lactose and casein, palm oil shortening is a good alternative.

Vinegar. Years ago vinegar was a confusing subject for the gluten-free. Current research has cleared all vinegars produced in the United States and Canada except malt vinegar. I use balsamic vinegar in all my cooking, even when it calls for another, just because I love the rich flavor. Balsamic vinegars are made from grapes that have spent at least 12 years aging in barrels of different types of aromatic woods. A little like aged wine, the older the vinegar, the more expensive it is.

In Italy most cooks have several vinegars: a light and younger one for salads such as a Modena, older thicker vinegar for topping risotto and fine fish dinners, and a special bottle, handed down, of thick molasses syrup-vinegar for the most exalted meals. For the recipes in this book, one good bottle of Modena or older balsamic is all you will need. After a little experimenting, I think you'll find the taste and age of a vinegar that best suits your palate. Like a good bottle of wine, it takes some exploration and is purely a personal affair.

Herbs. In professional cooking classes, they teach that the most important flavoring components are salt, pepper and fresh herbs. Throughout this book, my recipes are written for fresh herbs, and although you may substitute dry herbs in a pinch, using fresh herbs is superior. I have an herb garden that I use all summer and into the fall. In the winter I keep several pots of herbs in my house such as basil, parsley, oregano and rosemary. If you lack the room or a green thumb (although herbs are very easy to grow), local markets have a good selection of organic herbs. In the dead of winter when my pots have been picked bare, I will often buy a mix of fresh poultry seasonings, which have a little thyme, sage, oregano and rosemary — a terrific combination for savory soups or stews. There is always enough left over to use in my cooking throughout the week. Fresh basil and Italian flat-leaf parsley, which I use often, are available year-round in large fresh bunches. Keep them in your refrigerator with their stems in a glass of water, and you'll be surprised at how long they last.

Gli Antipasti
APPETIZERS AND SOUPS

Gli Antipasti

*T*he word antipasto literally means "before the meal." This whimsical course might consist of a platter of breaded artichoke hearts, a steamy bowl of minestrone soup or a plate of capicolla ham, olives, and roasted red peppers. It is typically a small dish that hints at the food to come, a mere tantalizing taste that prepares the gastric juices. Yet it's not a dish that should be overlooked. Small and unassuming, yet full of color and artistry, the antipasto is the course to set the mood. It piques the interest of the taste buds, and awaken the long lost joy of full dining that is often forgotten among those of us on restrictive diets.

Many of the *antipasti*, or appetizers, that follow are a combination of old family recipes with a new twist. You'll learn how to build an irresistible vegetable antipasto tray with lightly battered artichoke hearts, fried zucchini and roasted peppers. Or recreate family favorites such as baked stuffed artichokes, vegetable crostini and eggplant caponata. Recipes of savory meat and cheese wraps, with a bright marinade, and mussels in wine broth round out these first nutritious entrées.

And of course there are the soups. A pot of *minasta*, *pasta fagioli* or hearty minestrone can easily steal the show. With an herb focaccia, soup can become what the Italians would call a "peasant meal." The simple antipasto is a perfect balance of proteins, vitamins and "good" fats. It often combines meats with vegetables of the season garnished with pure extra virgin olive oil.

The antipasto is a worshiper of the seasons. In the summertime, I like to wander in my garden or along the streets of the farmer's market, picking the freshest produce and herbs, which I combine in a number of ways. In the winter, I often turn to the oven or stove to create a hearty soup partnered with a fresh focaccia. And there lies the beauty of this first course. With the antipasto, more than with any other part of the meal, you get to play, be creative, and use the foods your body craves.

Have fun with this section. Decorate your plate. Stimulate your eye with color and arrangement. Set the mood for the meal, or make it the center of your dining experience. In any case, an antipasto is a celebration of a glorious feast, a whisper of great things still to come.

Taking stock

What is the flavor missing in your cuisine? Why does your recipe fall flat compared to a restaurant's version, even if you copy it to the last detail? The answer will most likely lie in the secret of homemade stock. Stock is the foundation for most chefs' recipes, and a pot of simmering stock is a constant in restaurant kitchens.

The process of making stock is quite easy. So why do we resist? It takes time, and every cook (including me) will run out of that valuable commodity more than anything else. When you do have the luxury of time and are ready to make delicious homemade stock, there are three things you must know:

❧ Always use cold water to start your stock; this helps draw out the flavors from your meats and vegetables.

❧ Add a minimum of a *mirepoix,* a vegetable combination including carrots, onions and celery.

❧ Add a bouquet of these seasonings: thyme, bay leaves, sage, sea salt and black peppercorns.

The addition of other herbs or vegetables is your choice. I like to add fresh parsley, savory or marjoram simply because I have them in my herb garden.

There are two types of stocks. A white stock is made from poultry or meat bones that are unroasted. A brown stock is made from meat bones that are roasted in the oven. I will not be using a brown stock in this cookbook — since it takes some eight hours to make, I've decided to skip that recipe. Instead I've concentrated on vegetable stock, a simple garlic stock, and a traditional white poultry or meat stock. I like to use these in risotto, soups, pot pies, sauces, gravies and braised meat dishes. There is also a fish stock made from shrimp shells or lobster shells that takes less than an hour, and can be used in the seafood risotto. Each of these stocks can be made ahead of time and freeze quite well. One batch of stock can make a supply that will last for several recipes.

When you must rely on store-bought substitutions, there are a few good commercial broths. When choosing any commercial stock, make sure that you check the label for MSG, modified food starch or any seasoning additives that might have a gluten tag. I particularly like the flavor of Pacific Natural Foods® Mushroom Broth and French Onion Soup. Their Organic Beef and Chicken Stock are also adequate. All of these products are gluten-free. I tend to stay away from the bouillon cubes even if they claim to be gluten-free. They are often nothing more than flavored salt. You may have your own preference. Make sure to check the label, and call the company if you have any questions.

The safest and the best alternative is homemade stock. So the next time you are spending a few hours in your kitchen to create a beautiful meal, put your stock pot to use on a back burner and simmer away. You'll see just how easily you can improve the taste of your cuisine.

ANTIPASTO MARTINI

This show-stopping appetizer is really all about presentation. You can add thin slices of prosciutto cotto (baked ham) or spicy salami — or make it strictly a vegetarian affair. And because most everything can be purchased, assembly takes just minutes. Here's how I like to serve it:

Ingredients

¾ cup Parmesan cheese, grated

1 15 oz. can artichoke hearts packed in water, drained and quartered

1 large egg, beaten

½ cup Mary's Gluten-free Bread Crumbs (see page 80)

1 jar marinated roasted peppers, thinly sliced

2 TBL capers, drained

1 cup calamata olives or spicy Spanish olives

2 TBL balsamic vinegar

12 slices baked ham or salami such as Genoa, or thinly sliced pepperoni

8 oz. cheese such as provolone or cheddar, cut into ½" sticks, or shaved pecorino

DAIRY-FREE

Omit cheese sticks and Parmesan chips, and add your favorite rice crackers or gluten-free breadsticks.

MIX IT UP

PREHEAT OVEN TO 400 DEGREES, AND LINE A BAKING SHEET WITH PARCHMENT PAPER.

✎ To make Parmesan chips, sprinkle a generous tablespoon of grated Parmesan cheese on the prepared baking sheet, forming 12 circles about 2½" each in diameter. Bake in oven about 5 minutes, allowing cheese to melt together to form solid circles. Remove from oven, and cool slightly.

✎ Over medium high heat, add oil to a large skillet. Dip artichoke hearts in the egg and then the breadcrumbs, and place in hot oil. Cook until golden brown on each side, about 5 minutes. Remove to a plate and salt lightly.

✎ Mix the marinated peppers with the capers and set aside.

✎ In 6 martini glasses, layer ingredients one at a time, starting with a layer of peppers and capers. Then add a layer of artichoke hearts and top with olives.

✎ Roll each meat slice into a tight cylinder shape, or fold twice into a fan shape, and tuck into the rim of the glass. Add the cheese sticks to the rim, and then tuck 2 Parmesan chips into each glass rim. Add 2–3 olives on a toothpick to top off the martini.

Makes 6 martinis

MARY'S ANTIPASTO

Sundays with my family were full of relatives gathered around our large kitchen table. Starting at noon, we'd begin dining and would continue eating until early evening. Then we'd eat some more. This spectacular antipasto constituted our evening snack. Although it looks difficult, it takes only minutes to prepare. Yet with a special arrangement, a homemade marinade and garnish for presentation, it will start — or in my family's case, top off — any meal beautifully.

MIX IT UP

❧ Cut the prosciutto slices in half crosswise to create 24 long, narrow pieces, reserving half. Wrap 1 piece prosciutto around each of the 12 prepared cantaloupe wedges. Sprinkle lightly with fresh ground pepper.

❧ Lay the remaining prosciutto slices on a cutting board covered with parchment or wax paper. With a butter knife, spread each slice of prosciutto with 1 TBL of the mascarpone, leaving a ½" edge. Top the mascarpone with several arugula leaves. Place 1 asparagus spear on the edge of each prosciutto slice. Roll in a spiral until the prosciutto slice completely wraps it.

❧ Fold the ham and pepperoni slices in half, and then in half again, to form a triangle fold.

❧ Line up the mozzarella balls, basil leaves and cherry tomatoes on a cutting board. With the tip of a wooden skewer, add a cherry tomato, basil leaf and a mozzarella ball. Repeat, adding 2 layers of each per skewer.

❧ Place the olives in a small dish. Leave the cheese in a wedge, and serve with a cheese knife.

❧ When designing your antipasto tray, use a spiral design with a centerpiece of the dish of olives, the cheese wedge, or the asparagus stems set in a tall glass. Or, you could divide the tray into sections, placing the tomato, mozzarella and basil skewers in one triangle, the cheese or olives in the center, a triangle for each meat, and a pile of wrapped asparagus. It's up to you!

❧ For the marinade, mix the olive oil and balsamic vinegar, and then add the fresh minced herbs, minced garlic and salt and pepper. Whisk or shake the dressing, and sprinkle over the entire platter.

Ingredients

12 very thin slices prosciutto

1 cantaloupe, cut into 12 wedges, with seeds and rind removed

fresh ground pepper

12 fresh asparagus stems, trimmed and lightly steamed

4 oz. mascarpone, Italian cream cheese or regular cream cheese, softened

1 cup arugula leaves

½ lb. ham, thinly sliced

¼ lb. pepperoni, thinly sliced

30 fresh mozzarella balls

30 fresh basil leaves

30 cherry or pear tomatoes

1 cup marinated olives (black, green or a combination)

½ lb. wedge sharp cheese such as Grana Padano, Parmesan or Fontina

15 wooden skewers

Marinade

⅓ cup olive oil

3 TBL balsamic vinegar

2 tsp fresh herbs such as Italian flat-leaf parsley, basil or thyme

1 clove garlic, minced

salt and pepper to taste

Serves 8–10

Antipasto di Verdure

ROASTED VEGETABLE ANTIPASTO

I never fail to get compliments on my assorted roasted and sautéed vegetable antipasto. This beautiful dish combines the fresh tastes of the season with varied marinades and spices that make it irresistible. Add your favorite cheese and a fresh herb focaccia, and you can call this dinner.

Ingredients

Roasted garlic and peppers

1 bulb elephant ear garlic

2 red, orange or yellow peppers, cleaned and quartered

3 TBL olive oil

salt and pepper

Artichokes

2 TBL olive oil

¼ cup tapioca flour

1 large egg

salt and pepper

¼ cup Parmesan cheese, grated

1 15 oz. can artichoke hearts packed in water, drained and quartered

MIX IT UP

PREHEAT OVEN TO 350 DEGREES. LINE A BAKING SHEET WITH PARCHMENT PAPER OR LIGHTLY GREASE.

Roasted garlic and peppers: Remove skin from garlic cloves, and wrap in a tin fold pouch with 1 TBL of olive oil and a pinch of salt. Roast on a tray in the oven at 350 degrees for 40 minutes, turning once until garlic is soft.

🍃 Brush peppers with olive oil, salt and pepper, and lay skin side down on baking sheet. Bake for 15 minutes. Turn peppers and bake for another 10 minutes or until the peppers are easily pierced with a fork. Remove from oven and let cool.

Artichokes: Add olive oil to a large skillet and heat. Place tapioca flour in a bowl. Mix eggs and Parmesan cheese, salt and pepper in a second bowl. Dip artichokes in flour and then egg mixture, and add to hot oil. Without stirring, cook artichokes for about 5 minutes on each side or until golden brown. Remove to paper towel-lined plate, and sprinkle with salt and pepper.

continued

MIX IT UP *continued*

Sun dried tomato salad: In a small bowl, cover sun dried tomatoes with boiling water. Let hydrate for 30 minutes. When tomatoes are plump, drain water and return to bowl. Add olive oil, minced garlic, minced herbs and balsamic vinegar. Let marinate.

Squash: Heat oil in a skillet. Salt and pepper squash, and add to pan. Cook for 5 minutes, turn and add sliced garlic. Do not overcook garlic, or it will turn bitter. Add breadcrumbs. Sauté until the squash is easily pierced by a fork. Transfer to a platter with breadcrumb and garlic toppings. Sprinkle with Parmesan cheese and *Mary's Vinaigrette* (see page 153) if desired.

Serves 8–10

Ingredients

Sun dried tomato salad

8 sun dried tomatoes

¼ cup olive oil

1 tsp minced garlic

1 TBL herbs such as Italian flat-leaf parsley, basil or oregano, minced

1 TBL balsamic vinegar

Squash

2 TBL olive oil

1 medium squash such as zucchini or summer squash, sliced

¼ gluten-free bread crumbs

1 clove garlic, sliced

1 TBL Parmesan cheese, grated

Melanzane Ripiene
STUFFED EGGPLANT

Eggplant, or melanzane, appeared on our family table in many forms. We had breaded and fried eggplant for melanzane sandwiches. Sautéed eggplant topped our pizzas and spaghetti. Mrs. LaBarko made her famous Eggplant Parmesan in a jar — paper-thin eggplant layered in olive oil and garlic, lightly dressed with a fresh tomato sauce. Here's another classic eggplant dish, very thinly sliced eggplant dipped, floured and breaded, and then stuffed with a seasoned ricotta.

Ingredients

1 large purple globe eggplant, thinly sliced

3 TBL tapioca flour (more if needed)

1 cup gluten-free bread crumbs

2–3 eggs, beaten

olive oil

salt and pepper to taste

1 cup ricotta cheese

1 egg

¼ cup Parmesan cheese, grated

1 TBL Italian flat-leaf parsley, chopped

1 cup Capone's Marinara Sauce (see page 101)

DAIRY-FREE

Use *Mary's Dairy-Free Ricotta* (see page 113), or stuff the eggplant with a vegetable sauté such as the *Eggplant Caponata* (see page 31).

MIX IT UP

PREHEAT OVEN TO 375 DEGREES. LIGHTLY GREASE A 9x13" (OR SIMILAR SIZE) BAKING DISH.

❧ Slice the eggplant ¼" thick. Place in a single layer on paper towels and sprinkle with salt. Let stand for 30 minutes, and then blot moisture from the eggplant. This process removes excess moisture and also bitterness.

❧ Place tapioca flour and bread crumbs on two separate plates. Lightly beat 2–3 eggs in a medium bowl. Dust eggplant slices with tapioca flour, dip in egg and then pat onto plate of bread crumbs.

❧ Option 1: Frying: Heat olive oil in a large skillet. Fry eggplant until golden brown, about 3 minutes on each side. Place on a paper towel-lined plate.

❧ Option 2: Baking: Line two baking sheets with parchment paper. Place the breaded eggplant slices in a single layer. Drizzle oil over the top, and sprinkle with salt. Bake at 375 degrees until tender, about 15 minutes.

❧ In a medium bowl, mix together ricotta, egg, Parmesan cheese, parsley, salt and pepper.

❧ Place a small amount of the ricotta mixture, about 1½ TBL, in center of each eggplant slice. Roll the eggplant into a cylinder. Transfer to the prepared baking dish. Close the ends of the *ripiene* with a toothpick, or pack them tightly into the dish, with the opening of the cylinder facing the bottom of the pan. Cover the eggplant with sauce, and garnish with Parmesan cheese. Cover and bake about 20 minutes.

Makes 12–14 ripieni

30

THE WHEAT-FREE GOURMET

Caponata di Melanzane
EGGPLANT CAPONATA

Eggplant has a sponge-like texture that absorbs the flavors of the other ingredients around it. This dish, caponata, includes so many flavors that your mouth will sing! When choosing an eggplant, make sure the cap and leaves are firm and fresh, and that the skin is shiny and without brown spots. For this recipe, I recommend the oval-shaped eggplant since it has fewer seeds.

MIX IT UP

~ Slice eggplant 1" thick. Place slices in a single layer on paper towels and sprinkle with salt. Let stand for 30 minutes, and then blot moisture and excess salt from the eggplant. This process removes excess moisture and also bitterness. Cut into cubes.

~ In a large frying pan, heat oil until hot. Sauté eggplant about 3 minutes on each side or until brown. Drain on paper towels.

~ Add peppers and onions to the pan, and sauté until vegetables are *al dente*, or firm.

~ Lower the heat and add tomatoes, olives, capers, vinegar, fresh herbs, pine nuts, salt and pepper. Add cooked eggplant and simmer, letting the mixture reduce and thicken, about 15 minutes.

~ Let cool and refrigerate mixture for at least 1 hour to join the flavors.

~ Serve with gluten-free crackers or *Parmesan Cheese Chips* (see page 78).

Serves 8

Ingredients

1 lb. eggplant, cubed

1 red, orange or yellow pepper, seeded and cubed

1 large yellow onion, diced

2 large ripe tomatoes, chopped

½ cup calamata olives, pitted and chopped

2 TBL capers, drained

2 TBL balsamic vinegar

2 TBL fresh herbs such as Italian flat-leaf parsley, basil or oregano

salt and pepper to taste

¼ cup pine nuts

olive oil or canola oil

EGGPLANT, MOZZARELLA, TOMATO AND BASIL

Here's a new version of an old recipe using a tempura battered eggplant as the base of this fresh garden napoleon. For a lighter version, brush the eggplant with a little olive oil instead of egg, and grill for a few minutes on the outdoor grill or in the oven. Either way, this is a great-tasting and easy-to-make antipasto.

Ingredients

1 egg

3 TBL tapioca flour

salt and pepper to taste

½ cup gluten-free bread crumbs (optional)

2 Japanese or Chinese eggplants (long slender types), sliced ½" thick

½ lb. mozzarella, thinly sliced

2–3 medium tomatoes, thinly sliced

3 stems fresh basil, or enough leaves for one on each vegetable stack

2 TBL olive oil

1 TBL balsamic vinegar

DAIRY-FREE

Substitute an alternative mozzarella cheese.

MIX IT UP

PREHEAT OVEN TO 350 DEGREES. LIGHTLY GREASE A BAKING SHEET OR LINE WITH PARCHMENT PAPER.

Slice eggplant into ½" thick slices. Place slices in a single layer on paper towels and sprinkle with salt. Let stand for 30 minutes.

In a small bowl, mix together egg, tapioca flour, salt and pepper. Place gluten-free bread crumbs on a plate.

Dip eggplant slices into the egg tempura mixture, and then coat lightly with bread crumbs.

Heat olive oil in a skillet, and fry eggplant until golden brown, about 3 minutes per side. Transfer to a plate lined with paper towels. Salt lightly.

Transfer eggplant to platter and top hot eggplant with mozzarella slices, tomato and basil.

Drizzle with oil olive oil and balsamic vinegar.

Makes 12

STUFFED BACON-WRAPPED DATES

Bacon and fruit combinations are always a favorite on Italian tables. This version calls for the addition of a red wine reduction and is an easy and plentiful appetizer for those last-minute dinner parties.

MIX IT UP

PREHEAT OVEN TO 350 DEGREES. GREASE A SMALL BAKING DISH.

⮞ Cook bacon in a pan, leaving it slightly undercooked so that bacon is pliable and can be wrapped easily around the dates. Remove to a paper towel-lined plate and cool. Reserve 2 TBL of bacon grease in the pan.

⮞ Cut dates open on one side, leaving skin intact.

⮞ Mix together goat cheese and thyme.

⮞ Spoon about ½ tsp of goat cheese mixture into each date, and gently press closed. Cut bacon in half crosswise. Wrap one piece of bacon around each of the stuffed dates. Secure with toothpicks if necessary. Place in casserole dish.

⮞ Heat pan with bacon grease over medium high heat, about 1 minute. Whisk wine, vinegar and sugar into pan. Reduce until sauce thickens and forms a syrup, about 5 minutes. Pour over top of dates, and bake in oven for 20–25 minutes. Serve warm.

Makes 14–16

Ingredients

8 pieces bacon such as smoked apple bacon or pepper bacon

14–16 dates, pitted

4 oz. Cheves goat cheese

1 tsp fresh thyme, chopped fine, stems removed

¼ cup red wine

2 TBL balsamic vinegar

1 TBL sugar

DAIRY-FREE

Substitute soy cream cheese for goat cheese, and add a pinch of salt and pepper to mixture.

PANCETTA WITH HONEY GOAT CHEESE, FIGS AND THYME

I served this savory appetizer at a party I catered, only to have people grabbing pieces of sizzling pancetta right from the oven! This easy first course — with the combination of delicious Italian bacon, slightly sweetened goat cheese, figs and fresh thyme — is irresistible.

Ingredients

10 slices pancetta

10 oz. goat cheese

2 TBL honey

10 figs

1 TBL fresh thyme, stems removed

DAIRY-FREE

Substitute soy cream cheese for goat cheese.

MIX IT UP

PREHEAT OVEN TO 400 DEGREES. LINE A BAKING SHEET WITH PARCHMENT PAPER.

✎ Cut pancetta slices in half, and place them on the prepared baking sheet. Bake for 10 minutes or until pancetta is crispy.

✎ In food processor or blender, mix goat cheese and honey until creamy.

✎ Cut figs in half.

✎ Using a pastry bag with a flower tip, squeeze about 1 TBL goat cheese onto each cooked pancetta piece. Add a fig half, and sprinkle with thyme. Serve warm.

Makes 20 bite-sized morsels

Capesante alla Pancetta e Salsa d' Arancia

PANCETTA SEA SCALLOPS IN CITRUS GARLIC SAUCE

This dish is a combination of the sweet taste of lightly sautéed sea scallops in an orange garlic glaze, wrapped in savory pancetta. You can serve this as an appetizer or a main course on a bed of lightly sautéed spinach.

MIX IT UP

❧ Cut pancetta slices in half, and place them on the prepared baking sheet. Bake for 7 minutes or until pancetta is crispy but pliable.

❧ Rinse and dry sea scallops. Wrap a pancetta slice around the outer edge of the scallop. Close with a toothpick if necessary.

❧ In a large skillet, heat butter and oil over medium heat. Add garlic and cook for 2 minutes. Add scallops and sauté for 3 minutes on each side or until they are a light golden brown.

❧ Add orange juice, zest and Bragg's to the pan and cook with scallops, about 3 minutes.

❧ Transfer scallops, dividing them between plates. Gently simmer, whisking any drippings from the bottom. Reduce citrus sauce by half, about 5 minutes. Spoon sauce over the top, and sprinkle with sesame seeds.

Makes 6 appetizers or 3 main course meals

Ingredients

18 large sea scallops

9 pieces pancetta

1 TBL butter, ghee or butter alternative

1 TBL olive oil

1 orange, juiced and zested

1 clove garlic, minced

1 TBL Bragg's Liquid Aminos

1 TBL sesame seeds, lightly toasted

pepper to taste

Chef's Notes

I like to use gluten-free Bragg's Liquid Aminos for this sauce, although any gluten-free soy sauce will do. If you are soy-free, you can substitute 1 TBL of balsamic vinegar and a pinch of sea salt to make a nice reduction sauce.

Cozze in Brodo

MUSSELS IN SAVORY WINE BROTH

On Christmas Eve, my sister Camille carries on the tradition of preparing a full sit-down seafood dinner. She starts the feast with one of my favorite dishes, mussels in a savory wine broth. Simple to prepare and full of seafood flavors, this dish could easily be a main course when served with a side of crusty gluten-free bread.

Ingredients

4 dozen mussels such as Prince Edward Island Mussels or Green Lipped, scrubbed and debearded

8 TBL butter, ghee or butter alternative

1 large white onion, chopped

6 cloves garlic, chopped

1 14½ oz. can whole tomatoes, chopped

1 tsp sea salt

pepper to taste

1½ cups dry white wine

½ cup fresh Italian flat leaf-parsley

lemon wedges for garnish

Chef's Notes

For safe eating, store live mussels in refrigerator, and cover with ice or a damp cloth to keep moist. Discard any that will not stay closed after squeezing their shells shut, or if they have broken shells or an "off" odor. Don't forget to discard any mussels that do not open during the poaching process. They are not suitable for eating.

MIX IT UP

❧ To clean and debeard mussels, use a stiff brush and scrub mussels well under running water. Scrape shells with a knife to remove any marine growth, and tug beard toward pointed end to remove. Soak mussels completely covered in a pot of cold water for about 1 hour. After 30 minutes, change the water.

❧ In a large stock pot, melt butter over medium heat. Add onions and sauté for 3 minutes. Add garlic, and cook for about 2 minutes. Add chopped tomatoes with juice, wine, salt, pepper and ½ of the parsley, and bring to a gentle boil for about 5 minutes.

❧ Add mussels to stock pot and cover. Lower heat and steam until mussels open, about 7–10 minutes. Discard any that haven't opened.

❧ Divide mussels evenly between bowls. Add stock to each of the dishes.

❧ Garnish the rim of the bowls with remaining parsley and a wedge of lemon. Serve with a crusty gluten-free bread.

Makes 8 appetizers or 4 main course meals

Panelle

CHICKPEA FRITTERS WITH SWEET ONIONS AND SUN DRIED TOMATOES

Panelle is a chickpea flour fritter that boasts its origin from Sicily. More nutritious and tastier than rice flour, it resembles polenta in texture and consistency. And, like polenta, this fritter lends itself to additional flavors nicely.

MIX IT UP

LINE A BAKING SHEET WITH PARCHMENT PAPER.

🌊 Bring water to boil over medium high heat. Whisk Mary's Baking Mix and chickpea flour together, and add to the water a little at a time to prevent lumping. Stir in onions, tomatoes, salt, pepper and rosemary. Lower heat and cook together until mixture thickens, about 2 minutes. Spread mixture onto prepared baking sheet, and let cool completely, about 30 minutes.

🌊 Cut cooled mixture into 3x4" patties, and press 1 TBL of hazelnuts onto each top. In a large skillet, heat a ½" layer of olive oil. Using a spatula, add patty to oil and fry until crispy and golden brown, about 5 minutes. Turn once and cook for an additional 5 minutes. Remove and drain on paper towels. Salt and serve immediately: plain, with fresh ricotta, and/or *Capone's Mariana Sauce* (see page 101) for dipping.

Makes 18

Ingredients

¼ cup Mary's Baking Mix

1½ cups chickpea flour

3½ cups water

1 small sweet yellow onion such as Vidalia or Maui, chopped

¼ cup sun dried tomatoes, hydrated and finely chopped

1½ tsp sea salt, plus more if desired

¼ tsp fresh ground pepper

1 TBL fresh rosemary

1 cup hazelnuts, chopped

olive oil for frying

salt to taste

MUSHROOM AND OLIVE TAPENADE CROSTINI

Crostini is a simple Italian appetizer sure to please everyone. The only drawback is that you may have to share your bread with the WE people, or wheat-eaters. Or try serving these on gluten-free crackers.

Ingredients

8 slices of Our Daily Bread (see page 58)

4 oz. fresh wild mushrooms such as shitake, crimini or portabella

4 TBL olive oil, divided

1 small shallot, minced

salt and pepper to taste

1 TBL fresh Italian flat-leaf parsley

2 cloves garlic, minced

1 cup calamata, or black or green Provencal or Greek olives, pitted

1 TBL capers, drained

1 tsp fresh thyme

1 TBL lemon juice

MIX IT UP

For mushroom topping: Heat half the olive oil in a sauté pan over medium high heat. Add shallots and sauté for 2 minutes. Add mushrooms and sauté for 3–4 minutes. Add salt and pepper, parsley and garlic and cook for an additional 2 minutes. Remove from heat.

For olive tapenade: In a food processor, add olives, capers, thyme, lemon juice, and fresh ground pepper to taste to remaining olive oil and blend to make a paste.

Toast bread. Cut into triangles wedges. Spread 1 TBL olive tapenade on toast. Top with mushrooms and serve.

Serves 8

Carciofi con Pane e Salsiccia

AUNT CARMEL'S BAKED STUFFED ARTICHOKES

At holiday time, my family would greatly anticipate the arrival of Aunt Carmel and her covered casserole dish of baked stuffed carciofi. Since it was such a prized and well-loved dish, we'd often save it for the end of the meal, as a sort of dessert. The secrets of this tantalizing casserole are in the slow cooking of the artichokes and the tasty stuffing.

MIX IT UP

PREHEAT OVEN TO 400 DEGREES, AND HAVE ON HAND A 9x13" GLASS BAKING DISH.

❧ Wash the artichokes, and trim the thorns from the tips with kitchen scissors or a paring knife. Open the leaves to make room for the stuffing.

❧ In a small bowl, mix the bread, egg, cheese, sausage, parsley, salt and pepper until well combined.

❧ Divide the stuffing into four parts. Add a teaspoon of stuffing (in several places) to the outermost layers of the artichokes, pushing the stuffing down toward the bottom of the leaves. Repeat on the next layer until you reach the center of the artichokes.

❧ Add 1" of water to the baking dish. Place each stuffed artichoke, flat bottom down, in the casserole dish, and drizzle the olive oil over the top of artichokes. Cover the dish with a tight-fitting lid or foil.

❧ Bake 1–1½ hours. The artichokes will steam slowly, and the stuffing will form a light brown crust. Check water levels every half hour, and add water if needed to maintain a 1" level.

❧ Artichokes are done when the leaves pull away easily and the meaty inner layer of the leaf is soft. The base, or heart, should be tender and easily pierced with a fork or sharp knife.

❧ Remove from oven, and serve warm or at room temperature.

Makes 4

Ingredients

4 artichokes, washed with thorns trimmed

2 cups gluten-free bread, diced

1 egg

½ cup Parmesan cheese (optional)

½ lb. mild Italian sausage, casing removed, cooked and chopped into small pieces

1 TBL fresh Italian flat-leaf parsley, finely chopped

¼ tsp salt (more if not adding Parmesan cheese)

½ tsp fresh ground pepper

2 TBL olive oil

DOUBLE-STUFFED PORTABELLA MUSHROOM

Although I list this as an appetizer, multiply it by four and you will have a delicious vegetarian entrée. There are so many layers of flavors in this mineral-rich dish — your palate will have a hard time tracking them.

Ingredients

1 large portabella mushroom, including the stem

6 small mushrooms such as baby portabella, crimini or shitake

1 TBL olive oil

1 TBL butter

1 shallot, minced

2 cloves garlic, minced

¼ cup walnuts, finely chopped

1 tsp fresh thyme, stemmed and chopped

1 tsp fresh oregano, stemmed and chopped

salt and pepper to taste

¼ cup cooking sherry

¼ cup ricotta cheese

2 TBL Parmesan cheese, grated

¼ cup sun dried tomatoes, hydrated and chopped

½ cup Basil Pesto (see page 112)

olive oil and balsamic vinegar

MIX IT UP

PREHEAT OVEN TO 350 DEGREES. LIGHTLY GREASE A SMALL BAKING DISH.

☞ Remove stems from mushroom caps and wipe clean with a damp cloth. Wash stems in cold water, and trim and discard any rough or dark-colored ends. Set the large portabella aside, and mince the small mushroom caps and stems.

☞ In a large skillet, heat olive oil and butter. Add minced mushrooms, shallot, garlic, walnuts, thyme and oregano. Sauté over medium heat, allowing the liquid to reduce. Salt and pepper to taste. Allow mixture to become dry and paste-like, about 5 minutes.

☞ Add sherry; simmer and reduce, allowing almost all liquid to evaporate, about 3 minutes. Set aside.

☞ Combine ricotta and Parmesan cheeses with sun dried tomatoes.

☞ Place the large portabella mushroom cap in the baking dish. Layer with fillings, starting with the mushroom filling, then the ricotta filling, and finally the basil pesto. Drizzle with olive oil and balsamic vinegar.

☞ Bake loosely tented with foil for 20 minutes, or until mushroom cap is soft to the touch. Cut in quarters and serve warm.

Serves 4

DAIRY-FREE

Substitute *Mary's Dairy-Free Ricotta* (see page 113), and ghee or butter alternative for butter. Omit Parmesan cheese.

Chef's Notes

If you want to make bite-size appetizers, use baby portabella mushrooms. There will be enough stuffing to fill 2 lbs. of mushroom caps.

GARLIC SOUP STOCK

Here's a simple soup stock that is great when you want a clear broth full of subtle flavors. Garlic stock is a great base for vegetable soups, risotto and a variety of delicate sauces.

MIX IT UP

In a large stock pot, combine water, garlic, onion, herbs, salt and pepper. Bring to a boil, and then reduce to a simmer with the pot covered for 2 hours. Strain into a container, and salt to taste.

If storing for later use, cool containers in an ice bath in the sink before placing in refrigerator (up to 2–3 days), or freezer (up to 2–3 months.)

Makes 2 quarts

Ingredients

2 quarts cold water

2 heads garlic, skinned and smashed

1 large yellow onion, thinly sliced

1 bay leaf

2 sprigs fresh thyme

3 TBL fresh sage leaves

3 TBL fresh oregano or savory

salt to taste

6 peppercorns

THE GLUTEN-FREE ITALIAN COOKBOOK

VEGETABLE STOCK

A good-tasting vegetable stock is a stock I have trouble finding commercially. Instead, I make my own in large batches and freeze it for future use. From this flavored base, you can add your own favorite spices and vegetables, and then use it to create any number of mouth-watering dishes.

Ingredients

3 large carrots, chopped

6 stalks celery, chopped

3 onions, chopped

12–15 mushrooms, stemmed

2 parsnips, chopped

2 TBL olive oil

1 cup dry red or white wine (optional)

4 bay leaves

4 sprigs fresh Italian flat-leaf parsley

3 sprigs fresh thyme

5 leaves fresh sage

salt and pepper to taste

4 quarts cold water

MIX IT UP

Peel, trim and rough-cut the vegetables.

In a stock pot, heat the olive oil over medium heat. Add the *mirepoix* (carrots, celery and onions), and lightly caramelize, sautéing for 5 minutes. Add the mushrooms and parsnips; sauté about 3 minutes.

Add wine (optional) and reduce, about 5 minutes.

In a cheesecloth wrapper (tied tightly), add the bay leaves, parsley, thyme, sage, salt and pepper, or sprinkled directly onto the vegetables.

Fill the stock pot with 4 quarts cold water (several inches above the vegetable line.) It is important that the water is cold to absorb the best flavor. Bring to a boil, and then reduce immediately to a simmer. From this point on, never let the stock boil. Skim any impurities that rise to the surface of the broth. Do not stir, or you will mix impurities and fats back into the liquid. Keep adding water to the uncovered stock pot to maintain original 4-quart level. Simmer 1 hour.

Skim stock and then strain through a fine mesh strainer into storage containers. Do not press on vegetables or they may release residue.

If storing for future use, cool containers in an ice bath in the sink before placing in refrigerator (up to 2–3 days), or freezer (up to 2–3 months).

Makes 4 quarts

FISH STOCK

Making fish stock is quite simple and much quicker than other soup stocks. It requires fish bones and heads, or you may use a smaller amount of an actual fillet. Avoid using fatty fish such as salmon, mackerel or bluefish, since the flavor is too strong. Sole, monkfish, whitting, tilapia or turbot are best. You may also substitute the shells of lobster, crab or shrimp if you have the leftovers. Fish stock is great in soups, seafood risotto and seafood sauces.

MIX IT UP

➳ Rinse fish bones and heads, thoroughly removing any trace of blood.

➳ Add all the ingredients to a stock pot except the wine. Bring to a simmer over medium heat. From this point on, never let the stock boil. Skim any impurities that rise to the surface of the broth. Do not stir, or you will mix the impurities back into the liquid. Lower the heat and simmer for about 15 minutes.

➳ Add wine and simmer for another 15 minutes, skimming the surface frequently.

➳ Remove from heat (cooking longer than 30 minutes can make your stock bitter.) Strain through a fine strainer or cheesecloth, pressing the fish bones gently with the back of a wooden spoon.

➳ For mildest taste, use immediately. If storing, cool containers in an ice bath in the sink before placing in refrigerator (up to 2–3 days) or freezer (up to 2–3 months).

Makes 2 quarts

Ingredients

2–2½ lbs. flatfish bones and heads, or ½ lb. fish fillet

2 quarts cold water

1 small onion, sliced

1 small shallot, chopped

2 stalks celery, chopped

1 medium carrot, chopped

2 cloves garlic, peeled and smashed

2 bay leaves

6 peppercorns

2 sprigs fresh thyme

2 TBL or more sea salt to taste

⅓ cup dry white wine

POULTRY STOCK

Although you might find a usable commercial chicken broth, there is nothing comparable to this homemade version. I like to make this basic poultry stock when I'm preparing a meal that might leave me with bones and vegetables scraps.

Ingredients

3 large carrots, chopped

3 onions, chopped

6 celery stalks, chopped

4 sprigs fresh Italian flat-leaf parsley

4 bay leaves

3 sprigs fresh thyme

5 fresh sage leaves

salt and pepper to taste

3 lbs. bones or wings such as a chicken or turkey carcass, chicken or turkey wings, carcass chopped in pieces

1 cup dry white wine (optional)

4 quarts cold water or more, covering bones by 1"

MIX IT UP

⤜ Peel, trim and rough-cut vegetables. Set aside.

⤜ For the herbs and salt and pepper, either place in a cheesecloth wrapper (tied tightly), or sprinkle directly on the vegetables.

⤜ Add bones to stock pot. Add wine (optional), and reduce until wine is mostly evaporated, about 5 minutes.

⤜ Cover bones with cold water, and bring to a boil. Immediately reduce to a simmer. Never let the stock boil again (boiling will release the bone marrow into the soup and make stock cloudy.)

⤜ Add vegetables and herb pouch. Simmer uncovered for 2–3 hours. Every once in a while skim the fat and impurities off the top as it rises to the surface of the pot. Never stir the pot or the stock will be cloudy, as the fat will emulsify or mix together with your broth.

⤜ To produce a clear broth, continue removing impurities from the surface. Keep adding water when needed to maintain the original water level.

⤜ When finished, strain stock through a fine mesh strainer into storage containers. Do not press on the vegetables, or they may release residue. If storing, cool containers in an ice bath in the sink before placing in refrigerator (up to 2–3 days), or freezer (up to 2–3 months).

⤜ For general use in soups, stews, risotto and sauces, reduce this stock by one-third before using. Gently simmer and reduce stock for about 15 minutes, and then add to your recipes.

Makes 4 quarts

WEDDING SOUP WITH TURKEY MEATBALLS

I suspect this soup was served as the main dish for many a peasant wedding. Every Italian family has their own version of this meatball-laden dish, and each one is as delicious as the next. My version consists of turkey meatballs, a clear broth and seasonal vegetables. You can substitute ground chicken, beef, pork or lamb for your meatballs.

MIX IT UP: MEATBALLS

❧ In a small bowl, combine all ingredients and mix thoroughly.

❧ Roll into small individual meatballs about 1½" in diameter.

❧ Add to hot oil, and fry over medium heat until brown on all sides, about 12–15 minutes.

❧ Transfer to a plate and set aside.

MIX IT UP: WEDDING SOUP

❧ In a large soup pan, heat olive oil over medium to medium high heat. Add onion and sauté until translucent, about 3 minutes. Add carrots and celery; sauté until *al dente,* or light brown but firm, about 5 minutes.

❧ Add zucchini, bay leaf, thyme, sage, sea salt and pepper, and simmer about 3 minutes.

❧ Add broth and meatballs, cover loosely and simmer for 45–60 minutes, tasting broth periodically and adding salt and pepper to taste.

❧ Remove bay leaf before serving. Add a small amount of pasta to each soup bowl. Ladle with soup and several meatballs in each dish. Garnish with Parmesan cheese if desired.

Serve 6

Ingredients: Meatballs

1 lb. dark meat turkey, ground

1 egg

¼ cup gluten-free bread crumbs

¼ cup Parmesan cheese, finely grated (optional)

2 TBL fresh chopped herbs such as basil and/or Italian flat-leaf parsley

¼ cup chopped onion

½ tsp salt

¼ tsp pepper

1 clove garlic, minced

oil for frying

Ingredients: Wedding soup

2 TBL olive oil

1 large onion, chopped

2–3 carrots, peeled and diced

2 stalks celery with tops, diced

1 medium zucchini, diced

1 bay leaf

1 tsp fresh thyme

½ tsp dried sage

1 tsp sea salt

pepper to taste

6 cups of broth such as poultry, vegetable, garlic or beef

1 cup small gluten-free pasta, cooked

Zuppa di Cipolle e Funghi
SWEET ONION AND MUSHROOM SOUP

When the nights grow longer, I like to make this soup. A dark broth with mineral-rich mushrooms and onions filled with antiviral properties is a perfect way to feed your body in the changing season. Let this simmer for at least two hours to create a deep, rich flavor. For a beautiful finish, garnish each bowl with polenta croutons.

Ingredients

1 TBL olive oil

3 TBL butter, ghee or butter alternative

3 sweet yellow onions, very thinly sliced

½ lb. wild mushrooms such as shitake, porcini, oyster, crimini or morels

1 tsp or more salt

½ tsp sugar

1 TBL fresh Italian flat-leaf parsley, chopped

1 tsp fresh thyme, chopped

1 bay leaf

½ tsp fresh sage, chopped

3 TBL tapioca flour

8 cups broth such as beef, poultry, or onion broth, heated

½ cup dry white wine

salt and pepper to taste

Polenta Croutons (see page 79)

MIX IT UP

In a large saucepan, heat oil and butter. Add onions and cook covered over low heat, about 15 minutes.

Add mushrooms; cook over medium heat until mushrooms begin to take on color, about 10 minutes.

Stir in salt, sugar, parsley, thyme, bay leaf and sage. Cook uncovered for 30 minutes, or until onions and mushrooms are golden brown.

Add flour and stir. Cook about 3 minutes.

Add warmed broth and wine to vegetables; simmer partially covered for 30 minutes. Salt and pepper to taste.

Remove bay leaf before serving. Top with a sprinkle of chopped parsley, polenta croutons and/or Parmesan cheese as desired.

Serves 6

Chef's Notes

When choosing wild mushrooms, I love to explore flavors. Shitakes are full-bodied and have a meaty texture. Crimini or portabella are mild and wildly cultivated. Chanterelles are delicate but still full of woodsy flavor. Porcini are heady and meaty yet delicate enough for soups and sauces. Morels are prized for their superb earthy taste.

Minasta

ESCAROLE AND PEPPERONI SOUP

In my father's kitchen, there were always greens cooking on the stove. Dandelion greens, mustard greens and escarole made it to our plates in a variety of delicious forms. This soup version, with a spicy sausage added, is one of my favorites.

MIX IT UP

🍃 In a large stock or soup pot, heat olive oil and add onion. Cook until translucent, about 3 minutes. Add garlic, carrot, celery and pancetta. Sauté until vegetables are *al dente*, light brown but firm.

🍃 Add pepperoni or sausage to the vegetables. Sauté for 3–4 minutes.

🍃 Add broth, bay leaf, sage, thyme, salt and pepper. Simmer for 20 minutes.

🍃 Add escarole; simmer for an additional 10 minutes. Taste and adjust seasoning with salt and pepper.

🍃 Remove from heat. Remove bay leaf. Top with Parmesan or Romano cheese if desired and serve.

Serves 6

Ingredients

2 TBL olive oil

1 small yellow onion, diced

3 cloves garlic, smashed

1 large carrot, peeled and diced

2 stalks celery, diced

2 oz. pancetta or thick bacon, chopped (optional)

1 stick pepperoni or ½ lb. spicy sausage, cut into bite-size pieces

6 cups broth such as poultry, garlic or vegetable

1 bay leaf

1 TBL fresh sage, chopped (or 1 tsp dried)

1 tsp fresh thyme (or ½ tsp dried)

salt and pepper to taste

½ lb. fresh escarole

Parmesan or Romano cheese (optional)

Pasta e Fagioli

WHITE BEAN AND PASTA SOUP

Whenever I think of this soup, I see my Aunt Carmel stirring a pot of delicious pasta and beans. A version of this soup is found throughout Italy. I have taken the more traditional recipe and have made a white version for the Northern Italian palate. It's a simple soup loaded with light and crisp flavors.

Ingredients

2 TBL olive oil

1 TBL butter, ghee or butter alternative

1 small yellow onion, chopped

2 cloves garlic, minced

2 large carrots, peeled and chopped

2 stalks celery, chopped

4 cups chicken or vegetable broth

1 can of garbanzo or white cannelloni beans, drained and rinsed

1 zucchini or yellow squash, chopped

salt and pepper to taste

1 TBL fresh thyme, minced

1 TBL fresh sage, minced

2 bay leaves

1 cup gluten-free small dried pasta such as fusilli or elbow

Parmesan cheese, grated (optional)

MIX IT UP

🍃 In a Dutch oven or soup pot, cover bottom with a combination of olive oil and butter, and heat over medium heat. When oil is hot add onion, and sauté until translucent. Add garlic and simmer, about 3 minutes. Add carrots and celery; sauté for 5 minutes, or until vegetables are light brown.

🍃 Add broth, beans, squash, salt, pepper, thyme, sage and bay leaves.

🍃 Let simmer for 30 minutes, stirring and tasting to adjust flavors. Salt and pepper according to taste. When vegetables are tender but still firm, remove from heat. Remove bay leaves before serving.

🍃 Cook pasta, rinse and drain. Add a small amount to each bowl, and ladle soup on top. Garnish with grated Parmesan cheese if desired.

Serves 4–6

Minestrone con Riso

MINESTRONE WITH RICE

A good minestrone, or Italian vegetable soup, is a great way to start any respectable Italian dinner. This hearty recipe substitutes rice for the traditional pasta. Add a green salad and herb popovers, and this antipasto turns into a complete meal.

MIX IT UP

✎ In a large soup pot, heat olive oil/butter. Add onion; sauté until tender, about 3 minutes. Add carrots, celery and garlic. Cook for an additional 5 minutes or until vegetables are a light golden brown.

✎ Add zucchini, beans, potatoes, herbs, salt and pepper. Sauté for an additional 5 minutes.

✎ Lower heat and add tomatoes, green beans, broth and vinegar. Simmer covered for 1 hour.

✎ Add rice to soup just before serving. Remove bay leaves, and garnish each bowl with a tablespoon of Pecorino Romano or Parmesan cheese, if desired.

Serves 6

jIngredients

2 TBL olive oil, or 1 TBL oil and 1 TBL butter

1 small yellow onion, chopped

2 carrots, peeled and chopped

2 celery stalks, chopped

3 cloves garlic, minced

2 zucchini, diced

2 14 oz. cans beans, cannellini, or red kidney beans, drained and rinsed

2 potatoes, diced and peeled (optional)

¼ tsp red pepper flakes (optional)

2 bay leaves

1 TBL fresh thyme, chopped (or 1 tsp dried)

2 TBL fresh Italian flat-leaf parsley, chopped

1 TBL fresh sage, chopped (or 1 tsp dried)

salt and pepper to taste

4 large tomatoes, chopped (or 1 28 oz. can whole tomatoes, chopped with juice)

1 cup Italian flat green beans or regular green beans, cut into bite-size pieces

6 cups or more chicken or vegetable broth

1 TBL balsamic vinegar

1 cup rice, cooked

Pecorino, Romano or Parmesan cheese for garnish

Pane e Pizza

BREADS AND PIZZAS

Pane e Pizza

Breads, breads, beautiful breads

When visiting my grandmother's village in Pontelatone, Italia, I was sent to fetch the bread for dinner. Instead of going to a supermarket, which didn't exist, I followed a serpentine path down cobblestone alleyways to the back door of the town's bread maker. For what was the equivalent of 50 cents, I brought home a large, thick-crusted loaf of rustic Italian bread. *Delizioso!*

Bread is considered a staple of life, and with good reason. Bread is one of the oldest prepared foods dating back to the Neolithic era. It continues to be a fundamental food for cultures worldwide. Some of the world's best-loved breads come from France and Italy. The French practically live on a diet of crusty baguettes, and the Italians are renowned for their focaccia, panino bread rolls and hard-crusted pane. But what about a delicious loaf of gluten-free bread?

The art of making gluten-free bread

When I first began a gluten-free diet, I went to health food stores, ready to stock up on all the gluten-free goodies — especially bread — that I had seen lining the shelves. I tried loaf after loaf of gluten-free breads, only to chew on some dry, crumbling, gluey and tasteless concoctions. I found that commercial gluten-free bread no more resembled wheat bread than an old shoe. I immediately began experimenting in my kitchen to develop a good-tasting bread without gluten. A daunting task to be sure, since it is well known that gluten is a prized ingredient of any bread baker.

It took me years to create *Our Daily Bread* (see page 58), a basic recipe in honor of the pane from my grandmother's village. Like a loaf of rustic Italian bread, the texture is wonderful. Adding a variety of ingredients to the basic loaf will allow you to keep this bread new. Crunchy on the outside and soft and full of holes on the inside, *Our Daily Bread* stays together even when dipped directly in sauce. What more could you ask for?

If the thought of making gluten-free bread intimidates you, don't let it. With a simple balance of a good recipe, proper machinery and wholesome ingredients, you can enjoy baking wonderful bread again.

Tips for baking gluten-free breads

Let the machine do the work. I like to use a large capacity (9–11 cup) food processor to make dough, one that can handle 6–7 cups dry ingredients and 2½ cups liquids. For a single loaf, a smaller food processor will work. It must be able to mix at least 4 cups of dry ingredients and 1½ cups liquids. Alternatively, I also like to use a heavy-duty electric stand mixer, such as a Kitchen Aid, with a paddle attachment. A small hand-held mixer will not work either, since the motor is too weak for the stiff dough.

Even a large bowl and a wooden spoon will work, although it's a lot harder on the muscles. If mixing by hand, slowly add dry ingredients to wet, starting the mixing process with a whisk and then switching to a wooden spoon when dough thickens.

Since gluten-free bread is stickier than wheat flour bread, it is impossible to knead or mix with your hands. Adding more flour to the mix in order to handle it, like you might do with wheat flour dough, only results in a dense, gritty-tasting loaf.

Bread machines. I often get questions about bread machines. The problem is that most older bread machines have a second kneading function automatically built in. However, when making bread without gluten there is no benefit to a second kneading. When kneaded twice, gluten-free bread simply results in a denser loaf. However, there are many new machines with a gluten-free cycle that only kneads dough once. (See April 2008, *Living Without* that rates the best bread machines for gluten-free baking). When working with machines, I find it difficult to match the timing and baking results. Instead, I prefer to have more control over the bread by making my dough in a food processor or heavy-duty hand mixer, letting it rise in a warm area, and then baking it in the oven.

Proofing yeast. The first step in my bread-making process is to make sure the yeast is viable or active. The method I use in my recipes is called the "proof method." This method involves adding a teaspoon or two of sugar to commercial active dry yeast and warm water. Yeast is a living organism, so it's important to treat it as such. Adding sugar feeds the yeast.

Next, make sure the water is hot enough — but not too hot — to activate the yeast. I like to add water that is 110 degrees, gently stir, and then cover the bowl or measuring cup with a tea towel to keep the yeast mixture warm. If your yeast doesn't have a foamy head, about ¾" or more after 10 minutes, throw it out and start again. One of three things has occurred: your yeast has expired, the water temperature was too cold to activate the yeast, or too hot (over 115 degrees) and killed the yeast. No matter the reason, if your yeast doesn't work, your yeast bread won't work either. Start with new yeast, and use a thermometer to check your water temperature.

There is one recipe in this book that requires what is called the "sponge method." This method involves adding yeast to some liquid with a small amount of flour. Brown rice flour makes an excellent sponge, feeding the yeast well. A basic sponge can take from 30 minutes to 24 hours to mature. Sponges will result in evenly textured, full-flavored bread.

Kneading/mixing dough. Gluten-free dough is kneaded — or more accurately, mixed — only once. The more traditional method of kneading the dough twice belongs to wheat bread bakers. Gluten-free bread only requires a single mixing since the yeast is not feeding on gluten. The mixing process takes a different amount of time depending on which "machine" you use. When mixing by hand, this process will take about 10 minutes for the dough to form. With a heavy-duty stand mixer, it will take about 5 minutes. The food processor takes 2–3 minutes.

How can you tell when the dough has formed? When using a food processor, dough will begin to mound up in the center around the blade. When using a heavy-duty stand mixer, it will build up in the paddle. In either case, the dough pulls away from the edge of the bowl in ribbons or thick, thread-like strands (almost like a cotton candy threads) when ready.

Shaping dough. Your dough will resemble muffin batter or a thick cake batter with a little bounce when you touch it. It won't look like traditional wheat bread — and it's not supposed to. Once baked, this batter will turn into a golden loaf of delicious bread. After mixing, simply spoon the batter into your loaf pan, muffin pan or on a prepared baking sheet. Instead of trying to handle the dough by hand, I use a large spoon and a rubber spatula dipped in olive oil or water. If you really want to dive into the dough, you can use your hands dipped in oil or water. Shape the top of the bread smoothly, creating a tight surface, pinching or smoothing any cracks or seams together to close. Greasing the top with oil will allow for the dough to stretch while swelling during the rising process. When making focaccia, I spill the dough onto the prepared baking sheet and spread it out to the desired size and thickness with my wet hands or utensil dipped in oil. It's a little bit like working with very soft clay. When making pizza I spread my dough to ¼–½" thick and make a small lip at the edge of the crust to keep your toppings from spilling over.

Freezing and thawing dough. At this point, you may choose to freeze the dough to bake another time. After mixing and shaping the dough, double wrap it since freezer burn is a concern. I use an aluminum pan or a 9x5" loaf pan, wrap it in plastic wrap and then put the whole thing into a large freezer bag. If you are making rolls, place your dough on a parchment paper-lined tray that fits in your freezer, covered tightly in plastic wrap. Freeze completely and then transfer rolls to a freezer bag for easier storage. In a regular kitchen freezer, your bread will be good up to a couple of months. To thaw, transfer bread to the kitchen counter, allowing it to thaw completely in its wrapper to retain moisture. Then remove the wrapper and allow it to rise for up to 4 hours, or until it doubles in size. The cool temperature of the dough will require a slower proofing time.

Rising dough. Rising dough, also called proofing the dough, is the process by which dough transforms from a dense mass to a light and airy one. Dough can take anywhere from 40 minutes to 3 hours to proof, doubling in size. For the recipes in this book, I use a warming oven set at 80 degrees. If you don't have a warming oven, you can simulate one with the following method: Turn your oven on the lowest temperature for 3–5 minutes and then turn off the heat. Place the dough in the oven, allowing it to rise with the door ajar. I find that the warm oven helps to expedite the rising process, although it is not necessary for a successful proofing.

Placing dough on a kitchen counter or area that is about 75 degrees may take a little longer, but slower-rising dough makes a tastier loaf. The time the dough takes to rise will depend on the method you use. Just make sure that you don't allow the dough to rise more than 2–2½ times its original size.

You can also let your dough rise covered tightly covered with plastic wrap in the refrigerator for 8 hours, even overnight. Refrigerated dough must return to room temperature before baking, so return it to your kitchen counter to complete the rising process. Why use this

method? Letting dough rise in the refrigerator allows you to prepare the dough ahead of time and then remove it when you are ready. Then you can bake it before a party or an event where you want to be sure everything is fresh from the oven.

Scoring dough. Scoring dough with a sharp knife around the halfway point of the rising process allows the dough to expand further during the proofing and baking processes. It also adds a decorative design to the top of your loaf that can make your artisan bread even more artistic. Use a sharp serrated knife, slash the top no deeper than a ¼". You can use an "x" design on round loaves and rolls, parallel scoring on baguettes or long loaves, or a single slash down the center lengthwise on a sandwich loaf. It's totally up to you.

Glazing techniques. There are several glazing techniques that I recommend when making *Our Daily Bread* and its variations. The one I use most often is an egg wash, which is a whole egg beaten with a little water, or what the French call a *dorure*. This simple baker's varnish applied to the risen dough gives your homemade loaf that professional finishing touch. It also helps to adhere any seeds or toppings you might add to your loaf. Other washes include: eggs yolks with water, which results in a darker crust; beaten egg whites, which adds a shiny finish; and milk or cream for a dark and shiny finish. And of course there is the method of brushing the top with plain water several times during the baking cycle when making Italian or French crusty breads.

Xanthan gum. Don't forget this "glue" that holds gluten-free flours together. Once when I was baking rolls for an Autism Society gathering, I mixed my dough and noticed the constituency was more like crepe batter than bread. I decided I had not added the brown rice flour. So I added it, mixed it and still ended up with the same batter consistency. I finally realized I had forgotten xanthan gum! When I added the small amount required, mixed it — *presto*! A dough immediately appeared, although now it was extra thick. The moral of this story is: when your batter is not thickening, add xanthan gum. It can't hurt to add a little more, but you will definitely notice if you haven't added enough.

Baking the loaf. Place the bread loaf in the center of your preheated oven on the middle **or** lower rack to achieve the best browning of the bottom crust. Breads baked on a baking sheet should be placed in the center of the oven and baked one at a time, unless you have a good convection oven. Don't peek for the first 10 minutes, since this is the time that the yeast finishes releasing its gases, the bread expands to its maximum height and the final bread shape is formed. After that, you can open the oven to look, keeping in mind that heat is escaping.

Always check your bread 5–10 minutes before the recipe says it will be done. Only you and your oven will know the perfect time. Use your senses to determine when your bread is done. The first thing you should notice is the great aroma of freshly baked bread filling your kitchen. Next look at the color. Our Daily Bread or focaccia doughs are done when they are a deep golden brown not only on the top but on the sides as well. Finally, a loaf or roll should sound hollow when tapped on the bottom. If you are in doubt, use a cake thermometer to test the center for doneness. Temperatures for done centers can range from 180–220 degrees. I like to reach around 200 degrees. Every oven is different so times may vary a little. Becoming familiar with your own oven and timing are important elements to baking that perfect loaf of gluten-free bread.

Cool before slicing. When you have determined that your bread is done, remove it from the pan and immediately transfer it to a cooling rack. Your yeast bread is not technically finished until you have cooled it completely and the excess water has evaporated. A serrated knife used with a gentle sawing motion is the best way to cut homemade bread.

Storing bread. One of the most frequent questions I get is how to store homemade gluten-free bread. Like all breads made without preservatives, gluten-free breads will stay fresh for about three days either wrapped in plastic or foil, or in a bread box. After three days move bread to the refrigerator to keep it fresh for two more days. Whatever you don't consume in that time you might want to freeze to be thawed and toasted for another time. I find that 30 seconds in the microwave will easily refresh rolls or pieces of bread. You can enjoy them as is or toast lightly. I also like to use the leftovers to make valuable bread crumbs for any number of dishes. Just don't let your hard earned dough go to waste. If you can't eat the bread within five days, wrap the remains tightly in plastic wrap and then in a zipper-lock freezer bag and you will have bread or bread crumbs for another day.

Crepes, pie crusts, popovers and breadsticks

After you have mastered gluten-free bread, the rest is a piece of cake. Really. Simply follow the instructions in your recipes for each of the additional breads and crusts. A few things to note: for crepes, a crepe pan or non-stick skillet will greatly assist in the crepe-making process. For breadsticks, piping them through a pastry bag or a zipper-lock bag with the corner cut off gives them their signature shape. The secret to successful popovers is simply to preheat your muffin or popover pan in the oven before adding the batter. And finally, my chef's tips for a great gluten-free pie crust are to cool the dough sufficiently in the refrigerator and to use parchment paper when rolling it out.

CHEESE AND GARLIC BREADSTICKS

There's nothing like a light, airy cheese and garlic breadstick to make you forget you are on a limited diet. If fact, with this kind of bread you can eat like the Italians. Molto Bene! This dough starts cooking on the stove and then passes through a pastry bag. If you don't have a pastry bag, cut the corner of a large zipper-lock bag to the desired size.

MIX IT UP

PREHEAT OVEN TO 425 DEGREES. LINE 2 BAKING SHEETS WITH PARCHMENT PAPER OR LIGHTLY GREASE.

☞ In a medium saucepan, heat milk, butter, salt, pepper and nutmeg over medium heat until milk is scalded or forms a foamy surface ready to boil. Immediately add Mary's Baking Mix and xanthan gum to milk mixture and stir until dough forms. Cook for 3-5 minutes over low heat, stirring constantly.

☞ Pour the hot mixture into a food processor. Add egg, cheese and garlic; pulse until incorporated. The dough should be smooth and elastic.

☞ Spoon mixture into a pastry bag with a large, round tip. I like to use a #10 bag with the coupling attached and no tip. It's just the right size for breadsticks. If you don't have a pastry bag, use a large zipper-lock bag with the corner, about ½" trimmed off. Squeeze out long, thin mounds about 8–10" long and about a ½" in diameter. Use wet fingers to lightly press down the ends.

☞ Mix the beaten egg with the water. Brush the top of each breadstick with the egg wash, and sprinkle with toasted sesame seeds.

☞ Bake until golden brown, about 20-25 minutes.

Makes 18

Ingredients

1 cup milk

1 stick unsalted butter

1 tsp salt

dash pepper

pinch of fresh nutmeg

1 cup Mary's Baking Mix

2 tsp xanthan gum

4 large eggs

¼ cup Parmesan cheese, grated

1 egg, beaten

1 TBL water

2 cloves garlic, minced

¼ cup toasted sesame seeds

DAIRY-FREE

Substitute unsweetened milk alternative or water for milk; ghee or butter alternative for butter; and add 2 TBL fresh herbs such as thyme, parsley, rosemary and/or basil instead of cheese. For more flavor add 2 TBL minced onion flakes.

UR DAILY BREAD

It took me years to create this recipe to honor the memory of the great Italian breads of my youth. Like a loaf of Italian white bread, the texture is wonderful. It's spongy, moist and elastic, holding together nicely when toasted or even when dipped in sauce. Adding a variety of ingredients to the basic loaf will allow you to keep this bread new. Since this bread is without any preservatives, refrigerate any unused portion. Freeze unused portions or turn them into Mary's Gluten-Free Bread Crumbs.

Ingredients

2 tsp sugar

2¼ tsp active dry yeast

1½ cups warm water (about 110 degrees)

2½ cups brown rice flour

½ cup tapioca flour

¾ cup potato starch

4 tsp xanthan gum

1½ tsp salt

¼ cup olive oil

3 eggs plus 3 egg whites

1 tsp balsamic vinegar

1 egg

1 TBL water

MIX IT UP

PREHEAT OVEN TO 350 DEGREES. LIGHTLY GREASE ONE LOAF PAN WITH OLIVE OIL OR COOKING SPRAY. FOR DINNER ROLLS, LIGHTLY GREASE A 12-CUP MUFFIN TIN. FOR PANINO ROLLS, LINE A BAKING SHEET WITH PARCHMENT PAPER. FOR BOULE, LIGHTLY GREASE TWO 4" CAKE ROUNDS.

❧ In a small bowl, combine warm water, sugar and yeast. Stir just until dissolved. Cover with a kitchen towel and set aside in warm area for 10 minutes. Mixture will form a foam head about an inch. If mixture does not foam, your yeast is not viable or your water was too hot or too cold. At that point throw out your yeast mixture, and start again with fresh yeast.

❧ If using a food processor, add all dry ingredients: flours, xanthan gum, and salt, directly to the processor bowl. Blend in processor to mix flours together, about 3 minutes. If using a heavy-duty stand mixer, add to the mixer bowl, and mix with the paddle attachment for about 5 minutes until flours are well blended. If using a large mixing bowl, combine dry ingredients and whisk together until well combined.

❧ In another small bowl, whisk olive oil, eggs and vinegar until blended. Add egg mixture to dry ingredients and mix. Add yeast mixture to dough and mix.

❧ The kneading or mixing process takes different amounts of time depending on the machine you use. For mixing by hand, this process will take about 10 minutes. For heavy-duty stand mixer, 5 minutes. For those who use the food processor, it takes about 2–3 minutes for the dough to form.

continued

MIX IT UP *continued*

❧ When is the dough formed? When using a food processor dough will begin to mound up in the center around the blade. When using a heavy-duty stand mixer it will build up in the paddle. In either case, the dough pulls away from the edge of the bowl in ribbons or thick thready strands (almost like a cotton candy threads) when ready.

❧ Dough will be sticky and soft. Add one of *Our Daily Bread Variations* (see page 58) at this point. Gently stir just until combined.

❧ Transfer dough into prepared baking pan or muffin tin. For panino, shape batter into 3x4" football-shaped rolls. Smooth the top of the dough into desired shape with a spoon dipped in oil. (See "Shaping Dough," page 54.) Place in warm area to rise for 40 minutes. Dough will almost double in size. If using a warming oven, place baking pan inside uncovered, making sure temperature is not greater than 80 degrees. When finished rising, score and varnish top if desired. (See "Scoring Dough" and "Glazing Techniques," page 55.)

❧ For bread loaves bake for 40–45 minutes or 25 minutes, for dinner or panino rolls until crust is a golden brown and bread sounds hollow when tapped. (See "Baking the Loaf," page 56, to determine doneness.)

Makes one 9x5" loaf, 12 large dinner rolls, 8 panino (sub) rolls or 2 boules

Chef's Notes

The heat from the oven makes the gases in the dough expand, causing "oven spring," releasing moisture. Use a spray bottle to spritz the walls of the oven, or add a pan of water in to the oven to create humidity for a crisp, chewy crust. Sometimes I throw a handful of ice cubes in the bottom of oven several times during the baking process to create a burst of steam. Remember, don't open the oven for the first 10 minutes. See "Baking the Loaf" page 56, for complete instructions.

OUR DAILY BREAD VARIATIONS

To brighten this delicious textured bread, try these variations. After completing the Kneading/ Mixing Dough step (page 53-54), add one of the variations, and stir gently until just combined.

SUN DRIED TOMATO AND ROASTED GARLIC BREAD

Add ½ cup of hydrated sun dried tomatoes and a small roasted garlic (roast a head of garlic in the oven with ½–1" of top cut off and brushed with olive oil. Wrap in foil or roast on tray at 350 degrees for 40 minutes until garlic is soft. Let cool and remove skin.) Chop sun dried tomatoes and garlic coarsely. Add to prepared dough, pulsing only to blend. Score top and brush with olive oil instead of egg wash, and sprinkle with coarse salt or toasted sesame seeds, if desired.

ROSEMARY OLIVE BREAD

Add 3 TBL of chopped fresh rosemary or 2 TBL of dried rosemary and ½ cup of sliced pitted calamata olives. Add to prepared dough; pulse just until mixed. Score top. Brush with olive oil instead of egg wash, and sprinkle with coarse salt.

ITALIAN HERB BREAD

Add 3–4 TBL fresh rosemary, oregano, thyme, and/or basil (I like to use a combination) and 2 TBL Parmesan cheese. Omit cheese for a dairy-free variation. Add to dough and mix in thoroughly. Score and brush top with an egg wash or olive oil, and sprinkle with coarse salt or Parmesan cheese.

CINNAMON RAISIN BREAD

Mix together ½ cup dark brown sugar, 2 TBL cinnamon, ½ cup chopped walnuts and ¼ cup raisins (optional) in a small bowl. Add ¼ cup of the sugar mixture to the prepared dough; pulse until combined. Pour half of the batter into the prepared loaf pan. Add ½ cup of the remaining sugar mixture to the top of the batter. Using a cake or butter knife, gently swirl the batter and sugar together to create a marbled effect. Pour the remaining batter on top. Shape top with back of spoon and brush with an egg wash. Sprinkle with remaining sugar mixture.

SEEDED BREAD

Before placing bread in the oven, brush with an egg wash, and add this seed mixture to a dry skillet: 1 TBL minced garlic, 1 TBL minced onions, 1 TBL toasted sesame seeds, 2 tsp poppy seeds and ½ tsp sea salt. Toast lightly for about 1 minute. (Do not overcook or mixture will become bitter.) Sprinkle about ¼ cup of the mixture on top. Or, if you want to showcase one of the seasonings such as poppy seeds or toasted sesame seeds, use ¼ cup of the seeds and generously add to top of dough.

ONION AND CHEESE BREAD

Add ½ cup fresh, finely chopped onions and 1 cup coarsely chopped sharp cheese such as cheddar, Fontina, Swiss Emmenthal or Gruyère. Score top with several x's and brush with egg wash. Fill x's with an additional tablespoon of onions.

Ciabatta di Castagne
CHESTNUT CIABATTA

Ciabatta literally means "carpet slipper" because of its long, broad, and somewhat flattened shape. In Rome, this bread is often dressed with olive oil, salt and marjoram. Widely used as a sandwich bread, in this version of ciabatta, we use the sponge method to create a beautifully textured bread. The addition of chestnut flour gives it an extra nutty and rich flavor.

MIX IT UP: SPONGE

❧ Stir together yeast, sugar and ½ cup warm water. Let stand for 10 minutes until it is foamy. In another bowl, combine yeast mixture, flour, and xanthan gum. Stir for 3 minutes. Cover bowl with plastic wrap. Let sponge stand in cool temperatures for at least 12 hours and up to 24 hours.

MIX IT UP: CIABATTA

PREHEAT OVEN TO 425 DEGREES 15 MINUTES BEFORE DOUGH IS FINISHED RISING. LINE A BAKING SHEET WITH PARCHMENT PAPER.

❧ In a small bowl, combine warm water, sugar and yeast. Cover with clean towel or plastic wrap, and let sit for 10 minutes until foamy.

❧ In a food processor add sponge, yeast mixture, flours, xanthan gum, olive oil, salt and egg and mix until incorporated. Dough will be sticky.

❧ Turn dough out onto the prepared baking sheet. Form a loaf about a 9" oval, using a rubber spatula or your hands dipped in water or olive oil. Place covered in a warm draft-free area, or uncovered in a warming oven. Let rise for 1–1½ hours or until dough doubles in size.

❧ Bake ciabatta for 20–25 minutes or until a deep golden brown.

Makes one 9" loaf

Ingredients: Sponge

½ tsp active dry yeast

½ cup warm water (about 110 degrees)

1 tsp sugar

1 cup brown rice flour

½ tsp xanthan gum

Ingredients: Ciabatta

⅔ cup warm water (about 110 degrees)

1 tsp active dry yeast

1 tsp sugar

1 TBL olive oil

1 cup brown rice flour

¼ cup chestnut flour

¼ cup tapioca flour

2 tsp xanthan gum

1½ tsp salt

1 egg

MARIE'S CREPES

Marie's Crepes may be the most versatile recipe in this cookbook, since crepes are an excellent alternative to sandwich bread and make great desserts or even light pasta. This crepe recipe was handed down from an old German neighbor of mine and became a basis for my restaurant, Marie's Crepes. I've since converted it to a gluten-free version without any flavor or texture loss. Made ahead, these crepes can be refrigerated and reheated as needed.

Ingredients

¾ cup Mary's Baking Mix

1 TBL brown sugar

pinch of salt

4 large eggs

1 cup milk

2 TBL butter, melted

1 tsp gluten-free vanilla

DAIRY-FREE

Substitute unsweetened almond milk, soy milk or milk alternative for cow's milk; and ghee or butter alternative for butter.

MIX IT UP

☙ In a medium bowl, mix dry ingredients: Mary's Baking Mix, brown sugar and salt.

☙ In another bowl, mix eggs, milk and vanilla. In a 12" crepe pan, melt butter and add to egg mixture.

☙ Whisk egg mixture into dry until you have a smooth and silky texture.

☙ In a hot, lightly greased crepe pan or non-stick fry pan, pour just enough batter to cover the bottom of the pan (about ¼ cup), and swirl until batter reaches the edge of the pan. Cook until the edges start to pull away from sides and middle begins to firm, about 1 minute. Flip with a spatula, and cook on other side about 1 minute. Slide onto plate and repeat.

☙ Stuff with filling, and roll into tube or triangle shapes.

Makes 8–10

MARIE'S CREPE VARIATIONS

Here are some ideas for filling Marie's Crepes. Simply add a filling to the crepe after flipping it over the first time and cook for 1–2 minutes on the second side or until filling begins to warm and melt together. Fold crepe in half and then half again. Or if you prefer, roll it in a cylinder shape. Serve warm.

BREAKFAST CREPES

My favorite breakfast food is a Marie's crepe smothered with butter and pure maple syrup. When I am serving a special brunch, I make egg benedict crepes with a scrambled egg, diced ham filling and a hollandaise sauce over the top.

SANDWICH CREPES

Melt a slice of cheese and add ham or turkey to a crepe with a cream Dijon mustard, a curry mayo, or a condiment of your choice for a delicious lunch alternative. For a vegetarian sandwich, I like to add avocado, tomatoes, red onion and cream cheese. My daughters love a warm peanut butter and jelly crepe.

FRESH FRUIT CREPES

Add a sweetened cream cheese (cream cheese mixed with a little confectioner's sugar to taste) and your choice of fresh berries for a refreshing dessert or breakfast crepe.

CHOCOLATE CREPES

Add a gluten-free chocolate sauce or syrup or your favorite gluten-free chocolate chips to a crepe. Let them warm for 1–2 minutes and then fold or roll crepe. Chocolate chips will melt completely after folding.

JAM CREPES

For a traditional French dessert crepe, mix a little orange liqueur or cognac in your jam or preserves, and add 1 TBL to your crepe. Or if you prefer, simply use 1 TBL of your favorite jam.

CRÊPES SUZETTE

Prepare an orange butter by adding ¼ cup sugar to the zest of one orange. Cream sugar mixture into 1 stick of softened butter until fluffy, then beat in ⅓ cup orange juice and 2 TBL orange liqueur. In a chaffing dish, add butter mixture, and heat until bubbling. Dip both sides of cooked crepes in butter, fold and add to pan. Serve warm.

PARMESAN CHEESE HERB CREPES

Here is yet another use for Marie's versatile crepe recipe, a crepe pasta. This alternative to wheat pasta makes my Italian dishes light and delicious. Simple to make and easy to handle, these tasty crepes can be used in manicotti, cannelloni, or lasagna. The only problem is that they make such a light dish, you might find yourself eating more.

Ingredients

¾ cup Mary's Baking Mix

pinch of salt

2 TBL fresh chopped herbs such as a combination of Italian flat-leaf parsley, basil and oregano

4 large eggs

1 cup milk

2 TBL butter, melted

¼ cup Parmesan cheese, grated

DAIRY-FREE

Substitute plain almond, soy milk or milk alternative for the milk, and ghee or butter alternative for the butter. Omit Parmesan cheese, and increase salt to ¼ tsp.

MIX IT UP

☙ In medium bowl, mix Mary's Baking Mix, salt and herbs.

☙ In another bowl, mix eggs and milk.

☙ In a 12″ crepe pan, melt butter and add to egg mixture.

☙ Whisk egg mixture into dry until you have a smooth and silky texture.

☙ In a hot, lightly greased crepe pan or a 12″ non-stick fry pan, pour just enough batter to cover the bottom of the pan (about ¼ cup), and swirl until batter reaches the edge of the pan. Cook until the edges start to pull away from sides and middle begins to firm, about 1 minute. Flip with a spatula, and cook on other side, about 1 minute. Slide off onto plate and repeat.

Makes 8–10

Chef's Notes

These crepes can be made ahead of time and stacked on top of one another without sticking. If you are making them in advance, stack and wrap them in plastic wrap, and place them in a closeable baggie. They can be stored in the refrigerator up to 5 days.

Frittelle di Castagne
CHESTNUT PANCAKES

Chestnut pancakes can be served as a hearty breakfast cake or as a sweet bread with a savory meal. Try topping them with sour cream, cream cheese and fresh herbs, or your favorite jam or syrup.

MIX IT UP

❧ In a small bowl, whisk together milk and eggs.

❧ In a medium bowl, whisk together dry ingredients: flour, Mary's Baking Mix II, baking powder, brown sugar and salt.

❧ Add the wet ingredients to the dry, and whisk until well incorporated and batter is smooth.

❧ Heat griddle or skillet until a drop of water bounces off the surface.

❧ To make silver dollar-sized pancakes, ladle about 2 TBL of the mixture onto lightly greased griddle. Cook about 3 minutes per side.

❧ Transfer to a platter and dress with your favorite topping.

Makes 10

Ingredients

½ cup milk

2 large eggs

½ cup chestnut flour

½ cup Mary's Baking Mix II

2 tsp baking powder

2 tsp brown sugar

½ tsp salt

DAIRY-FREE

Substitute unsweetened almond milk, soy milk, milk alternative or water for milk.

accia

ITALIAN FLATBREAD

This Italian flat bread is a great companion to any meal. It's easy to make, and the dough is quite forgiving. In this recipe, I have added nutritious chickpea flour. Serve it with a saucer of olive oil mixed with salt and pepper or a bowl of sauce for dipping. It is my favorite recipe for pizza crust. The recipe can be doubled easily to make a larger loaf.

Ingredients

1 tsp sugar

1½ tsp quick-rising yeast

¾ cup warm water (about 110 degrees)

¾ cup brown rice flour

¼ chickpea flour

¼ cup tapioca flour

¼ cup potato starch

1½ tsp xanthan gum

1 tsp salt

3 TBL olive oil

2 eggs

½ tsp balsamic vinegar

2 tsp fresh rosemary, basil, or oregano, finely chopped (or 1 tsp dried)

Chef's Notes

Focaccia is super easy to make. You can even use a bowl and combine everything with a fork. Remember to use a rubber spatula or your hands dipped in water or olive oil to spread out your dough. I like to double the batch and freeze half in a double-wrapped freezer bag. (See "Freezing and Thawing Dough," page 54).

MIX IT UP

PREHEAT OVEN TO 400 DEGREES. LINE A BAKING SHEET WITH PARCHMENT PAPER OR LIGHTLY GREASE.

🍃 In a small bowl, combine warm water, sugar and yeast. Stir just until dissolved. Cover with a kitchen towel, and set aside in warm area for 10 minutes. Mixture will form a foam head about ¾".

🍃 If using a food processor, add all dry ingredients: flours, potato starch, xanthan gum and salt, directly into the processor bowl. Blend in processor, about 1 minute. If using a mixing bowl, combine dry ingredients, and whisk together until well combined.

🍃 In another small bowl, whisk olive oil, eggs, and vinegar until blended. Add egg mixture and yeast mixture to dry ingredients; mix just until combined.

🍃 Blend dough in a food processor for 2–3 minutes. (See "Kneading/Mixing Dough," page 53-54.) Dough will be sticky and soft. Add the ingredients for a focaccia variations at this point, and gently pulse or mix.

🍃 Transfer dough to the prepared baking sheet. Using a rubber spatula or your hands dipped in water or olive oil, shape dough into a rectangle or round shape about 1" thick for focaccia and ¼" thick for pizza. Place covered in a warm draft-free area, or uncovered in a warming oven, and let rise 40 minutes. Dough should double in size.

🍃 Preheat oven 400 degrees. Brush top with olive oil. Sprinkle with a pinch of coarse salt. Add your choice of seasoning, fresh herbs, or your favorite toppings. Bake 20–25 minutes or until light brown and crusty.

Makes one 9" loaf

Focaccia

ITALIAN FLATBREAD VARIATIONS

PIZZA CRUST

This Italian flat bread makes a great pizza crust. Simply follow the recipe for plain focaccia or any of the following variations, and shape the dough into a rectangular or round shape about ¼–½" thick. (See "Shaping Dough," page 54.) When shaping your dough, make a small lip at the edge of the crust to keep your toppings from spilling over. Remember, your dough will almost double in size so you can stretch it pretty thin. Add your favorite toppings to the risen dough.

PARMESAN CHEESE OREGANO FOCACCIA

Add ¼ cup finely grated Parmesan cheese and 2 TBL chopped fresh oregano or 2 tsp dried. Brush top with olive oil. Sprinkle with a pinch of coarse salt and 2 TBL Parmesan cheese.

FOCACCIA WITH ROSEMARY AND OLIVES

Add 2 tsp finely chopped fresh rosemary and ½ cup black olives, pitted and chopped, such as calamata or Italian olives in oil. Brush top with olive oil. Sprinkle with a pinch of coarse salt.

SUN DRIED TOMATO AND ROASTED GARLIC FOCACCIA

Add ½ cup sun dried tomatoes, hydrated in hot water and drained and chopped, and 6–8 cloves garlic, roasted and chopped. For roasted garlic, remove skin from garlic cloves and wrap them in a tin fold pouch with 1 TBL of olive oil added. Roast on a tray in the oven at 350 degrees for 40 minutes, turning over once until garlic is soft.

ONION AND CHEESE FOCACCIA

Add ½ cup fresh finely chopped onions and ¾ cup coarsely chopped sharp cheese such as cheddar or Fontina, Swiss Emmenthal or Gruyère. Brush with olive oil, and sprinkle with an additional tablespoon of onions.

CHESTNUT FOCACCIA

Substitute ¼ cup of chestnut flour and ¾ cup of brown rice flour for the 1 cup brown rice ingredient. Or for a richer chestnut taste, add ½ cup chestnut flour and ½ cup brown rice flour. Brush with olive oil, and sprinkle with a pinch of coarse salt.

Pizza Margherita

FRESH TOMATO AND CHEESE PIZZA

The margherita pizza is one of the most traditional pizzas of Italy. It's a simple collection of fresh ingredients: a crust covered with plum tomatoes and mozzarella cheese, and smothered with fresh herbs.

Ingredients

Add to one Focaccia recipe of your choice (see page 66)

¾–1 lb. fresh mozzarella cheese, thinly sliced

¼ cup Parmesan cheese, grated

¼ cup fresh basil, stemmed and chopped

2–3 plum tomatoes

fresh ground pepper

1 TBL or more olive oil

DAIRY-FREE

Substitute ½ lb. alternative mozzarella cheese, omit Parmesan cheese, and add a sprinkle of sea salt to the top.

MIX IT UP

PREHEAT OVEN TO 400 DEGREES. LINE A BAKING SHEET WITH PARCHMENT PAPER OR LIGHTLY GREASE.

✎ Prepare focaccia dough as directed. Transfer dough to baking sheet, and shape into a rectangular or round shape about ¼–½" thick. (See "Shaping Dough," page 54.) Place covered in a warm draft-free area, or uncovered in a warming oven, and let rise 40 minutes. Dough will almost double in size.

✎ Brush top of risen focaccia generously with olive oil. Add a layer of mozzarella, and then tomatoes to dough. Top it with basil leaves and fresh ground pepper. Sprinkle with Parmesan cheese.

✎ Bake for 20–25 minutes, or until toppings are melted together and crust is light brown.

Makes one 14" pizza

Quattro Stagioni
FOUR-SEASON PIZZA

The dairy-free four-season pizza is another of Italy's popular varieties. With this crispy pizza crust, you can use your imagination to create four distinctly different tastes. Kids like this version, especially when you let them decide how to decorate their very own quarter. Try cooking this one on a pizza stone to get the real Neapolitan effect. Here's my favorite combination.

MIX IT UP

PREHEAT OVEN TO 500 DEGREES. PLACE AN OVEN RACK IN THE LOWEST POSITION. LIGHTLY GREASE A PIZZA STONE, OR LINE A BAKING SHEET WITH PARCHMENT PAPER.

❧ Prepare Focaccia as directed. Sprinkle bottom of pan with cornmeal. Using a rubber spatula dipped in olive oil or with wet hands, spread the focaccia dough thinly on a prepared pizza stone or a baking sheet. Your final result should be about a 14" round pizza crust.

❧ Place covered in a warm draft-free area, or uncovered in a warming oven, and let rise 30–40 minutes. Dough will almost double in size.

❧ Add tomato sauce, and spread close to the edge allowing for a ½" crust.

❧ Divide the pizza into quarters and arrange the toppings: artichokes, prosciutto, olives and red pepper, into 4 sections. Add the fresh herbs and a drizzle of olive oil.

❧ Bake 20–25 minutes or until the crust is a deep golden brown. Cut and serve immediately with grated Pecorino Romano (if desired.)

Makes one 14" pizza

Ingredients

Add to one Focaccia recipe of your choice (see page 66)

1 cup or more of Capone's Marinara Sauce (see page 101) or tomato sauce of your choice

½ cup artichokes in water, drained and quartered

3 thin slices prosciutto

½ cup black olives such as calamata, pitted and sliced

1 red pepper, roasted and thinly sliced

1 tsp fresh basil, chopped

1 tsp fresh oregano, stemmed and chopped (or ½ tsp dried)

1 tsp fresh Italian flat-leaf parsley, chopped

olive oil

Pecorino Romano cheese (optional)

Chef's Notes

If you like a thin crust make sure you spread the dough as thin as it will stretch without holes. Remember your dough will double in size and will easily hold your ingredients.

Pizza Alla Mare

SEAFOOD PIZZA

My uncle "Zio" Joe made his seafood pizza by adding fresh tomato sauce and white anchovies with a drizzle of olive oil and Parmesan cheese grated over the top. I like to make mine with clams and a simple aglio e olio, or garlic and oil sauce, and, just for fun, I add capers to the mix. This simple-to-make pizza doubles as a delicious appetizer or a main course.

Ingredients

Add to one Focaccia recipe of your choice (see page 66)

¼ cup olive oil

¼ cup shallots, minced

3 cloves garlic, chopped

1 8 oz. can minced clams, juice reserved

2 TBL fresh Italian flat-leaf parsley, chopped

2–3 plum tomatoes, chopped

1 TBL fresh lemon juice

salt and pepper

2 TBL capers, drained (optional)

8 oz. mozzarella cheese

Parmesan cheese (optional)

red pepper flakes (optional)

DAIRY-FREE

Substitute ½ lb. alternative mozzarella cheese, omit Parmesan cheese, and add a sprinkle of sea salt to the top.

MIX IT UP

PREHEAT OVEN TO 400 DEGREES. LINE A BAKING SHEET WITH PARCHMENT PAPER.

☙ Prepare Focaccia as directed. Transfer dough to baking sheet and shape into a rectangular or round shape about ¼–½" inch thick. Place covered in a warm draft-free area, or uncovered in a warming oven, and let rise 40 minutes.

☙ In sauté pan, heat olive oil. Add shallots, and sauté about 2 minutes. Add garlic, and cook until garlic just begins to color, about 1 minute. Do not let garlic get too brown, or it will make your sauce bitter.

☙ Add minced clams and juice from the can, parsley, tomatoes and lemon juice. Salt and pepper to taste. Simmer on medium low heat for 20 minutes or until sauce is reduced by half.

☙ Add clam sauce to the prepared focaccia, and top with mozzarella cheese. Bake 20–25 minutes or until crust is a golden brown. Garnish with Parmesan cheese and red pepper flakes if desired.

Makes one 14" pizza

CAPONE'S DEEP DISH PIZZA

Deep dish pizza is truly an American creation. This version, with its reversed order of stacking the ingredients and slow cooking process, makes this pizza more of a torte. The cheese melts into the dough, the sausage cooks into the cheesy crust and the sauce conceals it all.

MIX IT UP

PREHEAT OVEN TO 350 DEGREES. LIGHTLY GREASE OR LINE WITH PARCHMENT PAPER A 10" SPRINGFORM PAN.

☙ Mix focaccia according to recipe and place in the springform pan. Place covered in a warm draft-free area, or uncovered in a warming oven, and let rise 40 minutes. Dough should double in size.

☙ On risen dough, first add a layer of mozzarella cheese, next the raw sausage, then the sauce, and finally add the Parmesan cheese and fresh herbs. This reversed layering prevents the cheese from overcooking and allows the meat to cook thoroughly while baking a longer time at a lower temperature.

☙ Bake 40–50 minutes until crust is brown and firm to touch. The center will be risen but soft to the touch.

☙ Remove outside ring of springform pan, and cut pizza into 8–12 slices.

Makes one thick 10" pizza

Ingredients

Add to one Focaccia recipe of your choice (see page 66)

½ lb. mozzarella, thinly sliced

½ lb. Italian sausage, casing removed

¾ cup Capone's Marinara Sauce (see page 101) or your favorite tomato sauce

¼ cup Parmesan cheese, finely grated

1 TBL fresh basil, chopped

1 TBL fresh Italian flat-leaf parsley, chopped

1 tsp fresh oregano, chopped

DAIRY-FREE

Substitute ½ lb. alternative mozzarella cheese, omit Parmesan cheese, and add a sprinkle of sea salt to the top.

Chef's Notes

Use parchment paper to line the entire springform pan. It will help protect against any scratches made from the cheese or sauce sticking to the sides.

Pizza con Funghi e Cipolle

MUSHROOM AND ONION PIZZA

A classic white pizza, Pizza con Cipolle, is often sold on the streets of Italy. I have added mushrooms and a balsamic sauce to this simple olive oil and onion topping for a little different flavor. This recipe makes a great bread or a dairy-free pizza.

Ingredients

Add to one Focaccia recipe of your choice (see page 66)

¼ cup olive oil

2 cloves garlic, chopped

½ cup sweet yellow onion, sliced

¼ lb. sliced wild mushrooms such as porcini, crimini, shitake, or oyster

¼ tsp coarse sea salt

pepper to taste

2 TBL balsamic vinegar

1 tsp sugar

2 TBL fresh herbs such as basil and oregano

MIX IT UP

PREHEAT OVEN TO 400 DEGREES. LINE A BAKING SHEET WITH PARCHMENT PAPER OR LIGHTLY GREASE A PIZZA PAN.

✎ Prepare focaccia dough. Transfer dough to baking sheet, and shape in rectangular or round shape ¼–½" thick. Place covered in a warm draft-free area, or uncovered in a warming oven, and let rise 40 minutes. Dough will almost double in size.

✎ In a large skillet, add olive oil, garlic and onion. Cook until translucent, about 3 minutes. Add mushrooms, salt and pepper, and sauté until mushrooms start to separate and turn a light brown, about 3 minutes. Add balsamic vinegar and sugar. Cook over medium low heat, caramelizing the liquid and reducing it by ⅓, about 3–5 minutes.

✎ Add mushroom and onion topping to risen pizza crust. Sprinkle with coarse sea salt and fresh herbs.

✎ Bake 20–25 minutes until crust is golden brown.

Makes one 14" pizza

Pizza con Pesto

PESTO PIZZA

Pesto makes a simple sauce for this tasty pizza variation. With the addition of fresh tomatoes and calamata olives, a cheese topping is really optional. If you choose to add cheese, a fresh cheves goat cheese and a Grana Padano, similar to Parmesan, combine to make a creamy and savory pizza topper.

MIX IT UP

PREHEAT OVEN TO 400 DEGREES. LINE A BAKING SHEET WITH PARCHMENT PAPER OR LIGHTLY GREASE A PIZZA PAN.

❧ Prepare focaccia dough. Transfer dough to the baking sheet and shape, with a rubber spatula dipped in oil, into a rectangular or round shape ¼–½" thick. Place covered in a warm, draft-free area, or uncovered in a warming oven, and let rise 40 minutes. Dough will almost double in size.

❧ In a large skillet, toast nuts until light brown and aromatic, about 3 minutes. Remove from heat.

❧ In a food processor or blender, add the pine nuts, Parmesan cheese, basil, garlic, olive oil, sea salt and pepper. Blend until mixed well, about 1 minute.

❧ Spread pesto sauce over risen crust. Add chopped olives and tomatoes to the top. Divide goat cheese over pizza top, and sprinkle with grated Grana Padano cheese.

❧ Bake 20–25 minutes until crust is golden brown.

Makes one 14" pizza

Ingredients

Add to one Focaccia recipe of your choice (see page 66)

1 cup pine nuts, walnuts, or hazelnuts

2 TBL Parmesan cheese

½ cup basil

1 clove garlic, chopped

¼ cup olive oil

sea salt and pepper to taste

½ cup calamata olives, pitted and chopped

1 ½ cups grape tomatoes, sliced in half lengthwise

4 oz. soft goat cheese

½ cup Grana Padano cheese, grated

DAIRY-FREE

Omit cheese and use a soy or almond mozzarella cheese substitute. Add a pinch of sea salt to the pesto and to top of pizza to brighten the flavor.

RAVEN'S PIZZA PIE

My daughter Raven created this rustic pizza which is a combination of her favorite ingredients. After the first bite, the family's only response was, "Yum!". Roasted peppers, caramelized onions, Italian sausage, sundried tomatoes, a little cheese and splash of sauce blend together to create a mouthwatering old world peasant dish fit for a queen.

Ingredients

Add to one Focaccia recipe of your choice (see page 66)

2 TBL olive oil

2 cloves garlic, chopped

½ cup yellow onion, sliced

½ lb. Italian sausage, casing removed

2 red, orange or yellow peppers, roasted and peeled

½ cup sun dried tomatoes, hydrated and sliced

1 cup mozzarella cheese, grated

1 cup Capone's Marinara Sauce (see page 101) or tomato sauce of your choosing

1 TBL fresh Italian flat-leaf parsley, chopped

salt and pepper to taste

MIX IT UP

PREHEAT OVEN TO 450 DEGREES, AND LINE A BAKING SHEET WITH PARCHMENT PAPER OR LIGHTLY GREASE A PIZZA PAN.

☞ Prepare focaccia dough. Transfer dough to the baking sheet, and shape into a rectangular or round shape ¼–½" thick. Place in a warm area to rise for 30–40 minutes. Dough will almost double in size. If using a warming oven, place inside uncovered, making sure temperature is not greater than 80 degrees.

☞ In a large skillet, add oil, garlic and onions and cook until translucent, about 3 minutes. Add sausage, salt and pepper; cook until brown, about 7–10 minutes. Break up sausage with the spatula into bite size pieces.

☞ Prepare roasted peppers and sun dried tomatoes (see *Roasted Vegetable Antipasto*, page 28.)

☞ Ladle marinara sauce over the top of risen focaccia dough. Add cheeses and sausage and onion mixture. Arrange sun dried tomato slices and roasted peppers. Sprinkle with parsley.

☞ Bake 20–25 minutes until crust is golden brown.

Make one 14" pizza

Chef's Notes

This pizza is great without cheese if lactose or casein is a problem. Buying the peppers and sundried tomatoes already prepared makes this a super easy supper.

Pizza di Patate

POTATO PIZZA

This Neapolitan recipe is another way to enjoy the simple pleasures of pizza. Using potatoes as a crust, you can add tomatoes, fresh mozzarella, prosciutto, and basil — or your favorite topping. The great thing about this pizza is that all parts are nutritious.

MIX IT UP

PREHEAT OVEN TO 400 DEGREES. LINE A BAKING SHEET WITH PARCHMENT PAPER OR LIGHTLY GREASE A 14" ROUND PIZZA PAN.

❧ In a large pot, boil potatoes with skin on until they are tender and can easily be pieced with a fork. Remove from water and let cool. Remove skin and push through food mill or the large side of a cheese grater into a large bowl.

❧ Add olive oil, Mary's Baking Mix, salt and pepper to potatoes, and stir gently until mixture is combined.

❧ Press potato mixture onto the baking sheet. Add a layer of tomatoes, then mozzarella cheese, prosciutto, basil and oregano. Finish with a sprinkle of Parmesan cheese and drizzle of olive oil.

❧ Bake 20–25 minutes until crust is brown on the edges.

Make one 14" pizza

Ingredients

1½ lbs. potatoes (about 4 medium potatoes)

¼ cup olive oil

¼ cup Mary's Baking Mix

½ tsp salt

pepper to taste

3–4 plum tomatoes, thinly sliced

½ lb. mozzarella cheese, thinly sliced or grated

4 thin slices prosciutto

2 stems fresh basil, stemmed and chopped

1 sprig fresh oregano, stemmed and chopped

¼ cup Parmesan cheese, grated

Chef's Notes

If you end up with more potatoes than the recipe calls for, add a little more baking mix. Boiling potatoes with their skins on help them from absorbing excess water.

DAIRY-FREE

Substitute ½ lb. alternative mozzarella cheese, omit Parmesan cheese, and add a sprinkle of sea salt to the top.

Pizzette

FRIED PIZZA DOUGH

As a kid, I waited all year for our Italian community's festival of Saint Michael's. It consisted of one city block filled with game booths, a shrine to Saint Michael, a bandstand for the older kids, and foods and confections galore. One of my favorite spots was the Scutter family booth that sold pizzette, or fried pizza dough, cooked on a Coleman stove. You can top this crisp dough with tomato sauce and a sprinkle of Parmesan cheese, mozzarella, ricotta, or butter and sugar.

Ingredients

¼ tsp yeast

⅓ cup warm water (105–115 degrees)

1 cup Mary's Baking Mix

½ tsp xanthan gum

¼ cup tapioca flour

pinch of salt

1 egg

1 tsp olive oil, plus oil for frying such as grape seed, canola, or olive oil

Chef's Notes

Pull dough gently by hand-shaping them into a small oval. An uneven thickness will create air bubbles when fried and will make a perfect pizzette.

MIX IT UP

❧ Dissolve yeast in warm water and let stand for 10 minutes. Yeast should form about a ½" foam head.

❧ In a food processor, combine Mary's Baking Mix, xanthan gum, tapioca flour, and salt. Pulse to mix.

❧ Gradually add the yeast mixture, and mix until you have a firm and slightly elastic dough.

❧ Shape into a ball, cover and let rise in a warm area for at least 1 hour.

❧ When dough has risen, roll dough into a long log about 1½" thick. Cut into 1" pieces and flatten with hands or with rolling pin into small discs. You may have to use a little Mary's Baking Mix to handle the dough.

❧ Cover the bottom of a heavy skillet with oil and heat. When oil is very hot, add discs of dough and fry, turning once when they are light brown and puffy, about 2–3 minutes per side.

❧ Blot excess oil on a paper towel. Add sauce or your choice of toppings. Serve immediately.

Makes 8 pizzetti

CRUSTY POPOVERS

One of my favorite bread recipes is the custardy, crisp popover. It's a great substitution for bread at any meal and is easy and rewarding to make. You can add herbs, meat drippings for Yorkshire pudding or make them plain, served with butter and jam. Popovers are another fantastic way to include breads in your diet.

MIX IT UP

PREHEAT OVEN TO 425 DEGREES.

Preheat a 12-cup muffin tin for 5 minutes. This is a very important step for popovers. A warm muffin tin helps to facilitate the rising of the batter. Let the tin stay in the oven until you are ready to pour in the batter.

In a blender, add eggs and milk. Pulse just until blended. Then add the tapioca flour, white rice flour and salt; pulse until combined.

Remove your baking tin (remember, it will be hot). Lightly grease with cooking spray. Pour in the batter, filling each muffin cup ¾ full. Fill any empty muffin cups with water to ensure even baking.

Bake 25 minutes, or until popovers are puffed high and are a rich, golden brown. For the puffiest popovers, avoid opening the oven door before 25 minutes. Serve immediately.

Makes 10

Ingredients

4 eggs

1 cup milk

⅓ cup tapioca flour

⅔ cup white rice flour

dash of salt

Variations

Garlic and herb popovers

Mix in after salt: 2 TBL fresh herbs (such as rosemary, basil, thyme, sage or a combination), stemmed and finely chopped, and 1 clove minced garlic.

Parmesan cheese popovers

Mix in after salt: ¼ cup finely grated Parmesan cheese and 1 TBL finely chopped fresh Italian flat-leaf parsley.

Yorkshire pudding popovers

Add 1 TBL of meat drippings to bottom of muffin cups before adding batter.

Chef's Notes

Over-mixing this batter will cause the popovers to be dense and more biscuit-like. A light touch with the blender will add just the right amount of air, creating a custard center and crisp crust. No peeking for 25 minutes.

DAIRY-FREE

Substitute 1 cup unsweetened milk alternative such as soy, almond or milk alternative for milk.

Parmesan Friscò

PARMESAN CHEESE CHIPS

The Parmesan cheese friscò is a distinctively cheesy cannoli that makes a great edible bowl or delicious chip. Simple to make, these sharp-tasting cannoli or chips add flavor to whatever you are serving. And they're fun to eat!

Ingredients

1 cup Parmesan cheese, coarsely grated

MIX IT UP

PREHEAT OVEN TO 350 DEGREES. LINE A BAKING SHEET WITH PARCHMENT PAPER OR SPRAY WITH COOKING SPRAY.

➤ **Parmesan cheese cannoli:** Sprinkle 3 TBL Parmesan cheese in a circle design on the baking sheet, leaving a little room to allow the cheese to melt together and spread. Repeat. Bake until cheese to melts together and forms solid circles, about 3–4 minutes.

➤ Remove from oven and wrap the warm cheese circles around a small rolling pin or other cylinder-shaped object, leaving an opening at the top to add stuffing. Another way to shape these disks is to drape the hot cheese circle over the back of a small bowl or mini muffin tin and allow to cool. These make great edible serving cups.

➤ **Parmesan cheese chips:** Add 1 generous TBL Parmesan cheese filling to baking sheet. Bake for 2 minutes or until circles are melted together. Remove from oven and let them cool flat.

➤ Serve with your choice of fillings.

Makes 6–8 cannoli or 16 chips

Crostini di Polenta

POLENTA CROUTONS

*Here is another great way to dress up your soups or salads with a delicious crunchy morsel.
I like to make my polenta croutons highly seasoned with fresh herbs or grated cheese, and salt
and pepper. Making a fresh batch of polenta will yield a large batch of croutons. But don't worry,
they freeze well.*

MIX IT UP

PREHEAT OVEN TO 400 DEGREES. LINE A BAKING
SHEET WITH PARCHMENT PAPER.

❧ In medium sauce pan, bring 1½ cups of water to
a boil.

❧ In small bowl, mix cornmeal, salt, and the
remaining ½ cup of cold water.

❧ Add cornmeal mix to boiling water, and lower heat
until the mixture stays at a moderate boil. Stir with a
wooden spoon almost constantly, about 25 minutes.
Polenta will thicken and begin to leave the sides of
the pan.

❧ Spread polenta on prepared baking pan lined with
parchment paper. Refrigerate until firm, at least 1 hour.
Polenta can be prepared up to 3 days in advance.

❧ Cut into 1" cubes. Bake 25 minutes until golden
brown and crisp. Serve as a topping for soups, salads or
vegetable dishes. Place any unused portion in closed
container and refrigerate or freeze with parchment paper
between layers. Reheat in oven before serving.

Makes 90 1" croutons

Ingredients

2 cups cold water, divided

*½ cup yellow or white finely ground
cornmeal (preferably stone ground)*

1 tsp salt

1 TBL butter, ghee or butter alternative

*1 TBL fresh chopped herbs such as
oregano, Italian flat-leaf parsley or
thyme*

*¼ cup Parmesan cheese, finely grated
(optional)*

MARY'S GLUTEN-FREE BREAD CRUMBS

I always take several slices of my gluten-free bread and offer them to the to bread crumb gods. I like to season my bread crumbs with herbs, but feel free to make them plain with salt and pepper, or with Parmesan cheese. I use bread crumbs on breaded cutlets, to top fish, to coat fried artichoke hearts, or to bread eggplant. Store them in an air-tight container in the freezer, and use just when needed for any recipe requiring that extra special, crumbly crunch.

Ingredients

2 thick slices gluten-free bread or 1–2 gluten-free rolls

2 TBL olive oil

salt and pepper to taste

2 TBL dried herbs such as parsley, basil, thyme or a combination (optional)

MIX IT UP

PREHEAT OVEN TO 350 DEGREES. LINE A BAKING SHEET WITH PARCHMENT PAPER.

➤ Cut bread coarsely, and pulse in a food processor until fine bread crumbs form.

➤ Move bread crumbs to a small bowl. Toss with olive oil, salt and pepper, and herbs and/or cheese if desired.

➤ Spread onto baking sheet, and bake until golden brown, about 20 minutes.

➤ Store in an airtight container for 4–5 days in the refrigerator, or up to 3 months in the freezer.

Makes 1 cup

SEEDED BREAD TOPPING

This lightly toasted combination of garlic, onions, sesame seeds and poppy seeds remind me of the Italiano bagels I once consumed in New York City. I use this as a topping for my gluten-free bread loaves, rolls and bread sticks. It can also be used as a fish or poultry seasoning, or as a topping for a vegetable dish. Sometimes my gluten-free, dairy-free, daughter uses this mix to replace Parmesan cheese.

MIX IT UP

In a medium skillet, add all ingredients and heat over medium heat until light brown, less than 1 minute. (Do not overcook or mixture will become bitter.)

Store in an airtight container, unrefrigerated, for up to 1 month.

Makes ½ cup

Ingredients

2 TBL minced garlic

2 TBL minced onions

2 TBL raw sesame seeds

¼ tsp coarse salt

3 tsp poppy seeds

Chef's Notes

Garlic will get bitter even if slightly over cooked so very lightly toast this mix. You can use fresh garlic and onion although I like to use dehydrated flakes when making this great topping.

I Primi

FIRST COURSE
PASTAS, RAVIOLI, GNOCCHI, SAUCES

I Primi

For the love of pasta

The undeniable, insurmountable center of every Italian table is the heaping bowl of pasta. My family's Sunday dinners were always inflated by a mountainous platter of spaghetti and meatballs, trays upon trays of manicotti, or a giant baking dish of bubbling lasagna. We'd all gather around our kitchen table...my Uncle *Zio* Joe, Aunt Carmel and Uncle Georgie, my parents, my five siblings and me.

When the pasta dish was served, the table would already be laden with loaves of crusty bread, a mixed green salad, and a massive hunk of Parmesan cheese. That gargantuan platter of pasta would loom like Mount Everest, humbling us all! Leaving food untouched on an Italian table rivaled a sin. Were we up to the challenge? Gripping our knives and forks, we steadied ourselves against the onslaught of the steaming pasta dish and dove in.

The word *pasta* literally means "paste." Originally, in its rudimentary state, it was a paste made from flour, water and salt. A fancier version emerged with the addition of eggs and was called "Sunday pasta." About 100 years ago, the pasta machine was introduced. Before that, the ancient knowledge of pasta making was handed down from mother to daughter, or in my case *zia* (aunt) to *nipote* (niece). Tables were laden with lofty mounds of flour, half a dozen eggs, warm water, a vessel of olive oil and a rolling pin — all that was needed to make the magical shapes of ravioli, tortellini, spaghetti, tagliatelle, lasagna and fettuccine.

In Italy, pasta is served in small portions as a *primo piatto,* or first course, always followed by a main course. When my husband and I first traveled to Italy, we were so enthralled with the first courses of so many enticing pastas and pizzas that we often ordered, to the shaking heads of our waiters, four *primi piatti.*

For most people, homemade pasta equals comfort food. For gluten-free dieters, homemade pasta is more akin to a kitchen miracle. Included in this book is a recipe for *Aunt Carmel's Homemade Pasta*, rightly named since I created it with the help of my Aunt Carmel, even though she passed on some 10 years ago. Let me explain. When I was writing this cookbook, I was struggling with what I considered to be one of the crowning recipes, homemade pasta. I was on my tenth version of this quintessential dish when I failed again to make the "paste" that formed the smooth, elastic mound I remembered as a child.

Out of frustration I let out a loud a cry. "Aunt Carmel," I wailed, "help me, please!" I was holding an egg in my hand at the time, ready to add it to yet another rendition of my flour

mixture, when all of a sudden my hand jerked quite forcefully. I lost almost exactly half of the egg.

Luckily, I was smart enough not to question what had happened. Instead, I added the remaining half of the egg and pulsed the paste in my food processor until it formed a perfect ball. I felt the consistency. It was good — something I was able to roll out and handle. And when I added it to the "boiling pasta pot," miraculously it held together.

The taste would surely tell if I had gotten it right. As I twirled the first forkful of pasta and set it to my mouth, I could hear my Aunt Carmel say, 'Tastes good, huh?'. I adjusted the recipe to contain a whole egg and the needed flour and aptly named it *Aunt Carmel's Homemade Pasta*. There you have it: the true story of my pasta recipe. Ancient knowledge handed down from beloved *zia* to *nipote*. From Aunt Carmel to me, and now to you.

The secret to making pasta

Whenever I mention making homemade pasta, most people roll their eyes and tell me that their pasta machine lies dormant in its original box tucked away in the back of a cupboard. I tell them to dust it off. The secret to gluten-free pasta making lies in your attitude. If you think making pasta is a struggle, it will be. If you approach it with love and the knowledge that your pasta making efforts will bring culinary delights to all that eat at your table, then you are ready to begin.

The assortment of brown rice flour pastas are dry pastas, and although they are edible and are a great offering to us gluten-free dieters, they are made mostly with rice bran and are often dense in flavor and tough in texture, not to mention tricky to cook. If hard pasta stays a minute too long in water, it turns to mush.

Fresh pasta is a totally different noodle. Nothing store-bought can compare with the soft, silky texture and fresh, aromatic taste of homemade pasta. Even if you find yourself covered in flour (rice flour of course) as you are busily crank away on your shiny pasta machine — smile. That is the true essence of Italian cooking. This is what my Aunt Carmel taught me. The love is in the dough.

Gluten-free pasta 101

Making gluten-free pasta is a little more challenging then making pasta with regular flour. Gluten-free pasta does not have the same elasticity as regular pasta dough, so don't expect it to feel the same. In a regular-flour preparation for pasta, there is a lot of kneading by hand and by machine, which stimulates the gluten to create more elasticity in the dough. When making gluten-free pasta, we skip this step since we will not increase elasticity with kneading; rather, we will handle our dough a little more gently. Lightly add only as much Mary's Baking Mix as necessary to handle the dough, and run it through the pasta machine only until it reaches the desired thickness.

To facilitate a happy pasta-making experience, have these things on board: pasta machine with desired heads, food processor, large wooden board (every Italian relative I know has one of these pasta boards in their kitchen), several large baking trays lined with parchment or wax paper and lightly dusted with rice flour, a bowl of Mary's Baking Mix nearby for your hands, a lucky apron, plastic wrap or tea towels.

1. Follow *Aunt Carmel's Homemade Pasta* recipe exactly, adding any desired variations as indicated. If you add even a tablespoon too much water, the dough will be sticky and hard to handle. If you add too much flour, it will be stiff and fall apart in the rolling-out process. If you follow the recipe your dough will have a consistency resembling, yes, play dough: pliable but not too sticky, soft and supple with a little elasticity. If the dough is too dry, add ½–1 tsp water and blend in a food processor. If it is too wet and sticky, use a little Mary's Baking Mix on your rolling pin and your hands. Dough consistency is everything. If you can't get it right after these adjustments, don't get frustrated. Throw it out and start again — the pasta is worth it!

2. Turn dough onto a lightly rice flour-dusted cutting board and shape it into a 4" disk (about the size of a saucer). Dough should be pliable but not sticky to touch. Cover with plastic wrap, and let rest for 30 minutes.

3. Cut into 8 pie-wedge pieces. Flatten each with a lightly dusted rolling pin or by hand, making each a rectangle the size of a playing card, about 3x4".

4. Using an electric or hand-crank pasta machine, feed the pasta ribbons into the widest setting, #1. Make sure your dough is thin enough to run through the widest setting. If your dough breaks up as it goes through the first time, gather the pieces, re-roll it more thinly and try again. Once you have run it through the first time, you will have successfully completed making the pasta ribbon. Next, fold the pasta ribbon in half, end to end, and run it through the widest setting one or two more times. You final ribbon will approximate a thickness of ⅛–¹/₁₆".

5. Place dough ribbons on a baking sheet lined with parchment paper and lightly dust with Mary's Baking Mix. Cover with plastic wrap. Continue rolling out remaining dough. When all the dough is rolled, uncover ribbons on baking sheet and let stand to dry for 30 minutes. Drying the noodles slightly helps with the handling and cutting of the ribbons into pasta noodles.

6. For ravioli, lightly brush pasta ribbon with an egg wash (1 egg beaten with 1 TBL water). Add 1 TBL filling in the middle of the pasta ribbon every few inches. Be careful not to overstuff, or they will be hard to seal. You should end up with 4 large ravioli per strip. Brush another pasta ribbon of similar size with the egg wash and place over the top of the strip with the filling. Using your fingers, gently press around the filling to seal it in. Cut edges with a pastry roller using the beveled edge or cut with a sharp knife. Your finished size will be around 3x4". For tortellini: cut a 1½–2" circle out of the dough, using a small glass or cookie cutter. Brush each circle of dough with an egg wash. Place about ½ tsp filling in the center of the circle. Using clean, dry fingers fold the pasta in half and press the edges together, sealing. Move with a spatula to another lined and lightly rice flour dusted tray. Repeat with the remaining pasta ribbons. With a slotted spoon or by hand, gently add ravioli or tortellini to salted boiling water and cook for 7 minutes, or until firm but tender. Remove with a slotted spoon and drain completely.

7. For cut pasta (fettuccine, linguini, spaghetti and tagliatelle), add the attachment to a pasta maker for your final cut. Fettuccine cutters make ½" wide noodles. Linguini, spaghetti or tagliatelle cutters form ¼" noodles. Feed the pasta ribbons through the machine. Place

noodles on a parchment-lined baking pan and dust noodles with a tiny bit of Mary's Baking Mix or rice flour to keep them from sticking together, tossing them gently with you hands to separate them. Cover with a kitchen towel, and let dry slightly for 1 hour or more. Add pasta to salted boiling water and cook for 2–3 minutes, or just until tender. Taste a strand of pasta often to determine doneness. Pasta should be firm and tender. Drain and top with sauce. There is no need to rinse the pasta since there is no rice bran in this mix.

8. Pasta can be used fresh, or you can dry it or freeze it for future use. For drying pasta, lay strands in a single layer on a baking sheet or drying rack and air-dry overnight. Store in an airtight container until used. For freezing pasta, let pasta noodles air-dry for one hour and then dust with rice flour and freeze in a plastic zip-lock bag lined with parchment paper. Noodles can be clumped into little "nests" that will come apart when cooked.

Suggested roller settings for Kitchen Aid attachment and most pasta makers:

#1	basic pasta ribbon dough
#3	egg noodles
#3–4	fettuccine, spaghetti, ravioli, lasagna
#5–6	tortellini, fine linguini
#7–8	angel hair, capellini

The sauces

I have to give a special credit to my relatives for the sauces that lend themselves to a gluten-free, and often dairy-free, diet. In this section, we will learn how to make the scrumptious *Capone's Bolognese* sauce, a richly flavored meat sauce. *Capone's Marinara*, unlike conventional marinara sauces, does not require all day to cook and is perfect every time. The creamy white sauces, *Capone's Béchamel* for cannelloni or lasagna, and *Alfredo Sauce* for fettuccini, are as simple as they are delicious. Seafood sauces such as the *Capone's Marinara with Lobster* and *White Clam Sauce* burst with the fresh taste of the sea. There are bright vegetable sauces such as *Salsa Norma*, and *Salsa Alla Marcella*, direct recipes from Italy, which are a perfect combinations of late summer produce. The *Lemon Artichoke Sauce* is simple and sensational for a last minute party.

All the sauces, save the white sauces that tend to separate, can be made ahead of time and stored in the refrigerator for 3–4 days. They also can be frozen quite easily for several months. Actually, I think that Italian sauces get better with a few days of age. I have given my suggestions on sauces with pasta dishes, but the choice is yours. Mix and match your sauces with pastas, and discover for yourself the full and rich possibilities of gluten-free Italian cuisine.

AUNT CARMEL'S HOMEMADE PASTA

One of my favorite childhood memories is of my Aunt Carmel making homemade pasta on a large wooden board in her meticulous kitchen. She'd start with a lofty pile of flour with a well in the center, to which she would add eggs, a dash of salt and a magical splash of water. Within minutes, using only her hands and a rolling pin, she had made perfectly even, thin fettuccine noodles piled high on the floured board. She'd always say a pasta machine would slow her down, and I believe it would have. For this basic, gluten-free egg noodle pasta, I use two machines — and I need them both!

Ingredients

1 ¼ cup Mary's Baking Mix

¼ cup tapioca flour

1 tsp xanthan gum

½ tsp salt

2 extra large eggs

1 TBL olive oil

1 ½ TBL warm water

Variations

For spinach pasta: *pulse ½ cup chopped and dried spinach with dry ingredients.*

For basil pasta: *pulse 3 TBL fresh chopped basil with dry ingredients.*

For black pepper pasta: *pulse 2 tsp fresh ground black pepper with dry ingredients.*

MIX IT UP

❧ Add Mary's Baking Mix, tapioca flour, xanthan gum and salt to a food processor and pulse.

❧ Add eggs, oil, and water. Mix until dough forms a moist ball.

❧ Transfer dough to a cutting board lightly dusted with Mary's Baking Mix, and shape dough into a 4" disk using as little extra Mary's Baking Mix as necessary. Dough should be pliable but not sticky to touch. Cover with plastic wrap, and let rest for 30 minutes.

❧ Cut into 8 parts. Flatten each with a rolling pin lightly dusted with Mary's Baking Mix or by hand, making each a rectangle the size of a playing card. Cover any unused portions with plastic wrap.

❧ Using an electric or hand-crank pasta machine, feed the pasta ribbons into the widest setting, setting #1. You have created a pasta ribbon. Fold the pasta ribbon in half, end to end, and run it through a few more times. Adjust the machine to a desired narrower setting, putting dough through 2 more times. The thickness is up to you and the cooperation of your pasta dough. Dough needs to reach a thickness of about ⅛–¹/₁₆".

❧ Try these settings for a Kitchen Aid® with a pasta attachment or most other pasta machines. The final settings will vary from machine to machine.

• Fettuccine: setting #1 then #4

• Tortellini: setting # 1 then #3 or #4

• Ravioli: setting #1 then #3

• Lasagna: setting #1 then #4 or #5

continued

Uncle Georgie and Aunt Carmel

MIX IT UP *continued*

❧ After running the pasta ribbons through the 2 desired settings, place dough ribbons on a baking sheet lined with parchment paper and lightly dusted with rice flour. Cover with plastic wrap. Continue rolling out remaining dough. When all the dough is rolled, uncover ribbons and let stand to dry for 30 minutes.

❧ If you are making lasagna, ravioli or tortellini, you are finished. If you are making noodles such as spaghetti, linguini or fettuccine, add the proper attachment to your pasta maker. Cut dough ribbons to desired length of noodles and feed them through the machine. Place noodles on another parchment-lined baking pan, and dust noodles with a tiny bit of Mary's Baking Mix flour, gently tossing them with your fingers to keep from sticking together. Cover pasta with kitchen towel, and let dry slightly for 1 hour or more.

❧ Add pasta to salted boiling water and cook for 2–3 minutes for fettuccine and 2 minutes for spaghetti, linguini or capellini, or just until tender. Taste a strand of pasta often to determine doneness. Pasta should be firm but tender. Drain and top with your favorite sauce.

Makes 1 lb.

Chef's Notes

This recipe needs to be followed exactly for a good dough consistency. Since egg sizes vary greatly, so will the consistency of your dough. For best results, use extra large eggs. Your finished pasta dough should feel like a soft modeling clay. If the dough is too dry, add ½–1 tsp water and blend in a food processor. If it is too wet and sticky, use a little of Mary's Baking Mix for your rolling pin and on your hands. Dough consistency is everything. If you can't get it right after these adjustments, don't get frustrated. Give the dough ball to your kids to play with, or throw it out and start again. The pasta is worth it!

Pasta Alle Castagne

CHESTNUT PASTA

On Thanksgiving, my father roasted a large platter of chestnuts to add to our already enormous feast. In Italy, century-old chestnut groves blanket the countryside, and at their peak season, chestnuts appear in dishes everywhere. In autumn, piping-hot chestnuts are sold on the streets or they are served up in home kitchens in meat and poultry stuffing. Castagnaccio is a treasured chestnut cake. In honor of the versatile chestnut, I decided to create a pasta recipe with a finely ground chestnut flour called Farina di Castagne, available on the internet and in specialty stores. This pasta is rich and slightly sweet like the nut itself. I like to use the narrowest attachment to make spaghetti or cappellini with this dough and then top it with a hearty White Bean Bolognese (see page 108), Capone Bolognese (see page 102) or a simple Capone's Marinara (see page 101).

Ingredients

¾ cup Mary's Baking Mix

½ cup chestnut flour

¼ cup potato starch

1 tsp xanthan gum

2 large eggs

1 tsp salt

MIX IT UP

❧ Add dry ingredients: Mary's Baking Mix, chestnut flour, potato starch, xanthan gum and salt to a food processor and pulse.

❧ Add eggs and mix until dough forms a ball or until the dough is elastic.

❧ Transfer dough to a cutting board lightly dusted with Mary's Baking Mix, and shape it into a 4" disk using as little extra Mary's Baking Mix as possible. Dough should be pliable but not sticky to touch. Cover with plastic wrap, and let rest for 30 minutes.

❧ Cut into 8 parts. Flatten each with a rolling pin lightly dusted with Mary's Baking Mix or by hand, making each a rectangle the size of a playing card. Cover any unused portions with plastic wrap.

❧ Using an electric or hand-crank pasta machine, feed the pasta ribbons into the widest setting, setting #1. Fold it in half, end to end, and run it through a few more times. Adjust the machine to a narrower setting (#4 is best), and put dough through 2 more times.

continued

MIX IT UP *continued*

❧ Place dough ribbons on a baking sheet lined with parchment paper and lightly dusted with Mary's Baking Mix. Cover with plastic wrap. Continue rolling out remaining dough. When all the dough is rolled, uncover ribbons on baking sheet.

❧ Add the spaghetti, cappellini or fettuccine attachment to your pasta maker. Cut dough ribbons to desired length of noodles and feed them through the machine. Place finished noodles on another parchment-lined baking sheet and dust noodles with a tiny bit of Mary's Baking Mix, gently tossing them with your fingers to keep from sticking together. Cover pasta with kitchen towel, and let dry slightly for 30 minutes or more.

❧ Add pasta to salted boiling water and cook 2-3 minutes or just until tender. Taste a strand of pasta to determine doneness. Pasta should be firm but tender. Drain and top with your favorite sauce.

Makes 1 lb.

Chef's Notes

Gluten-free chestnut flour is available on the web. It is primarily imported from Italy where they take gluten-free quite seriously. Check to see that it contains the words "Sensa Glutina" on the package to make sure it was milled in a gluten-free facility. Like other nut flours, it requires refrigeration after opening.

Ravioli Al Formaggio e Spinaci

CHEESE AND SPINACH RAVIOLI

I grew up eating these delicious ravioli and would anticipate with delight the warm, oozing cheese filling. Top this dish with Capone's Marinara Sauce (see page 101), Capone's Bolognese Sauce (see page102) or your favorite sauce. These are even great in brodo; in your favorite broth.

Ingredients

Add to Aunt Carmel's Homemade Pasta (see page 88)

1 cup ricotta cheese

2 TBL Parmesan cheese

2 TBL fresh Italian flat-leaf parsley, chopped

½ cup spinach, cooked and finely chopped

pinch of nutmeg

1 egg

salt and pepper to taste

1 egg beaten with 1 TBL of water for egg wash

Meat variation

Add ½ cup cooked Italian sausage, finely chopped, to the filling.

DAIRY-FREE

Substitute 1½ cups of *Mary's Dairy-Free Ricotta* (see page 113) for ricotta.

MIX IT UP

❧ Mix together ricotta, Parmesan, parsley, spinach, nutmeg, egg, salt and pepper in a small bowl.

❧ Make dough for *Aunt Carmel's Homemade Pasta*. Let rest for 30 minutes.

❧ Cut into 8 parts. Flatten each with a rolling pin lightly dusted with Mary's Baking Mix or by hand, making each a rectangle the size of a playing card. Cover any unused portions with plastic wrap.

❧ Using an electric or hand-crank pasta machine, feed the pasta ribbons into the widest setting, setting #1. Fold it in half, end to end, and run it through a few more times. Adjust the machine to desired narrower setting, putting dough through 1–2 times more. For making ravioli, the dough needs to be thin but pliable, at about setting #3 or #4. You should end up with eight 8x4" pasta ribbons.

❧ Place dough ribbons on a baking sheet lined with parchment paper and lightly dusted with Mary's Baking Mix. Cover with plastic wrap. Continue rolling out remaining dough. When all the dough is rolled, uncover the ribbons on baking sheet and let stand to dry for 30 minutes.

❧ Brush a pasta ribbon with the egg wash. Add 1 TBL filling in the middle of the pasta ribbon every few inches. Be careful not to overstuff the ravioli, or they will be hard to seal. You should end up with 3 per strip, depending on the size of your pasta ribbon.

continued

MIX IT UP *continued*

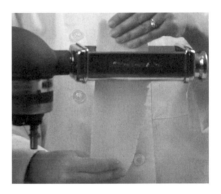

❧ Brush another similar-sized pasta ribbon with egg wash, and place over the top of the strip with the filling. Using your fingers, gently press around the filling to seal. Cut edges with a pastry or ravioli cutter using the beveled edge. If you don't have a cutter you can use a knife. Your finished size will be around 3x4". Move ravioli with a spatula to another baking sheet lined with parchment paper and lightly dusted with Mary's Baking Mix. Repeat with the remaining pasta ribbons. Let ravioli dry for about 30 minutes.

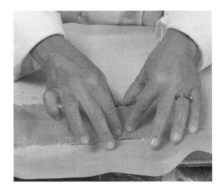

❧ With a slotted spoon or by hand, gently add to boiling salted water and cook for 7–10 minutes or until firm but tender. Remove with a slotted spoon, and drain completely.

❧ Top with your favorite sauce.

Makes 12–15 ravioli

Chef's Notes

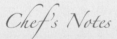

Try to make the pasta ribbons a similar size so they line up well. If you have holes or tears in the ribbon, add a patch with the extra dough. Do not overstuff your ravioli or they won't seal correctly and you'll lose your filling in the "bubbling pasta pot."

Agnolotti di Zucca

PUMPKIN TORTELLINI WITH BROWN BUTTER SAGE SAUCE

Whenever I make this delicate dish, I am transported back to a remarkable dinner I had on the Island of Murano near Venezia. A jolly, robust red-headed Italian served us fresh pumpkin filled large tortellini, sometimes called agnolotti, finished with a simple butter-sage sauce and accompanied by a white vino di casa from his family vineyard. Fantastico! Although you can use canned pumpkin if you are in a hurry, fresh pumpkin is superior in taste and texture.

Ingredients: Filling and dough

Add to Aunt Carmel's Homemade Pasta (see page 88)

1 small pumpkin (or 1 cup canned 100% pumpkin puree)

¼ cup Parmesan cheese

2 TBL fresh Italian flat-leaf parsley, chopped

¼ tsp allspice

1 egg

pinch of nutmeg

salt and pepper to taste

1 egg beaten with 1 TBL of water for egg wash

Ingredients: Sauce

6 TBL butter

¼ cup fresh sage leaves

Parmesan cheese for garnish

MIX IT UP: FILLING AND DOUGH

PREHEAT OVEN TO 350 DEGREES. LINE A BAKING SHEET WITH PARCHMENT PAPER OR LIGHTLY GREASE.

 Cut pumpkin squash in quarter wedges, remove seeds and place flesh side down on baking sheet in oven. Bake 30–40 minutes until flesh is tender. Remove 1½ cups pumpkin from the skin, and pulse in a food processor or blender until pureed. (If you are using canned pumpkin, place directly in the food processor or blender.)

 Add Parmesan, parsley, allspice, egg, nutmeg, salt and pepper, and blend just until incorporated.

 Make dough for *Aunt Carmel's Homemade Pasta.* Let rest for 30 minutes.

 Cut into 8 parts. Flatten each with a rolling pin lightly dusted with Mary's Baking Mix or by hand, making each a rectangle the size of a playing card. Cover any unused portions with plastic wrap.

 Using an electric or hand-crank pasta machine, feed the pasta ribbons into the widest setting, setting #1. Fold it in half, end to end, and run it through a few more times. Adjust the machine to desired narrower setting, putting dough through 1–2 times more. For making tortellini, the dough needs to be thin but pliable (try setting #3 or 4).

 Place dough ribbons on a baking sheet lined with parchment paper and lightly dusted with Mary's Baking Mix. Cover with plastic wrap. Continue rolling out

continued

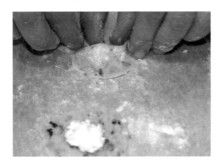

MIX IT UP *continued*

remaining dough. When all the dough is rolled, you are ready to make tortellini.

🥢 Using a small glass or cookie cutter, cut a 1½–2" circle out of the dough for half-moon shaped larger tortellini or agnolotti. Trim the remaining dough. Set the scraps aside, covering with plastic wrap.

🥢 Brush each circle of dough with an egg wash.

🥢 Place about ½ tsp filling in the center of the circle. Using clean, dry fingers fold the pasta in half, and press the edges together, sealing. Try not to overlap the pasta more than once or it will make the tortellini tough. Move tortellini with a spatula to another baking sheet lined with parchment paper and lightly dusted with Mary's Baking Mix. Repeat with the remaining pasta ribbons. Let tortellini dry for about 30 minutes.

🥢 With a slotted spatula or by hand, gently add tortellini to boiling salted water. Cook for 7–10 minutes or until firm but tender. Remove with a slotted spoon and drain completely. Transfer to serving platter.

MIX IT UP: SAUCE

🥢 Melt butter in a small skillet over medium heat. Add sage leaves, and simmer until butter begins to turn a light brown color. Remove and pour over cooked tortellini. Garnish with Parmesan cheese and serve.

Makes 30 large tortellini or agnolotti

DAIRY-FREE

Substitute ¼ cup of toasted pine nuts or toasted walnuts for Parmesan cheese. Increase salt to taste.

Chef's Notes

You may have to add a drop or two of water to revitalize dough scraps. You can reroll them and send them through the pasta machine again. If dough breaks up too much, toss it out.

Ravioli ai Fungi

GIANT MUSHROOM RAVIOLI

This wild mushroom mousse makes a delicate filling for homemade pasta, and can be served with the lightest sauces such as a Brown Butter and Sage Sauce (see page 94), a butter and Parmesan cheese sauce, an aglio e oli (garlic and olive oil) sauce, or a simple marinara.

Ingredients

Add to Aunt Carmel's Homemade Pasta (see page 88)

2 egg whites

½ tsp salt

pinch of pepper

¼ cup heavy cream or half-and-half

1 TBL olive oil

¼ cup walnuts, chopped

4 oz. chopped wild mushrooms, such as shitake, porcini, oyster or crimini

2 TBL combined oregano, thyme, basil and parsley, chopped

¼ cup Parmesan cheese

1 egg beaten with 1 TBL water

DAIRY-FREE

Substitute Silk creamer for heavy cream or half-and-half. Increase walnuts to ½ cup. Add a clove of minced garlic.

MIX IT UP: FILLING

🍃 In a food processor, add egg whites, salt and pepper and whip for about 2–3 minutes until egg whites begin to stiffen. Add cream in a slow, steady stream, pulsing to create a mousse.

🍃 In a sauté pan, heat oil. Add walnuts, mushrooms, herbs, salt and pepper to taste. Sauté for 3–5 minutes until mushrooms begin to brown.

🍃 Add mushroom mixture and Parmesan cheese to mousse. Pulse until blended and minced.

🍃 Refrigerate for 30 minutes before using.

MIX IT UP: PASTA

🍃 Make dough following the instructions for *Aunt Carmel's Homemade Pasta*. Let rest for 30 minutes.

🍃 Follow instructions for making ravioli ribbons and for filling pasta (see page 85-87).

🍃 Using your fingers, gently press around the filling to seal. Cut edges with a pastry or ravioli cutter using the beveled edge or a shape knife. Your finished size will be around 3x4". Move ravioli with a spatula to another baking sheet lined with parchment paper and lightly dusted with Mary's Baking Mix. Repeat with the remaining pasta ribbons. Let ravioli dry for 30 minutes.

🍃 With a slotted spoon or by hand, gently add to salted boiling water. Cook for 7–10 minutes or until firm but tender. Remove with a slotted spoon, and drain completely. Top with your favorite sauce.

Makes 12–15 large ravioli

Cappelletti in Brodo
TORTELLINI IN BROTH

This simple and light meal will delight the entire family. Cooked in a homemade stock or your favorite soup stock, this delicious stuffed pasta can be quite simple. I like to stuff these with a little gluten-free ricotta and some cooked meats such as chicken, beef or pork. It's a great way to use your leftover meats.

MIX IT UP

In a food processor add cooked meat and parsley. Pulse until finely minced. Add ricotta cheese, Parmesan cheese, egg, nutmeg, salt and pepper. Mix until smooth; set aside.

Make dough for *Aunt Carmel's Homemade Pasta.* Let rest for 30 minutes. Follow instructions for making pasta ribbons for *tortellini.*

Using a small glass or cookie cutter, cut a 1–1¼" circle for this smaller tortellini called *cappelletti.* Trim the remaining dough and set the scraps aside, covering with plastic wrap.

Brush each circle dough with an egg wash.

Place about ¼ tsp filling in the center of each circle. Using clean, dry fingers, fold the pasta in half and press the edges together to seal. Be careful not to overlap the pasta since it will make the cappelletti tough along the edges. Wrap the half circle around your index finger, and press the two ends together to form a ring.

In a 6–8 quart sauce pan, bring broth to boil and add cappelletti. Cook until *al dente*, about 7–10 minutes. Garnish with Parmesan cheese if desired, and serve immediately.

Makes 30 tortellini

Ingredients

Add to Aunt Carmel's Homemade Pasta (see page 88)

¾ cup or 6 oz. chicken, turkey, beef or pork, cooked and chopped

2 TBL fresh Italian flat-leaf parsley, chopped

½ cup ricotta cheese

1 cup Parmesan cheese, grated, plus more for garnish

1 egg

1 pinch nutmeg

salt and pepper to taste

1 egg beaten with 1 TBL of water for egg wash

6 cups chicken, vegetable or beef stock

DAIRY-FREE

Substitute ½ cup gluten-free bread crumbs and ½ cup toasted pine nuts for Parmesan cheese. Use *Mary's Dairy-Free Ricotta* (see page 113) for ricotta cheese.

Gnudi

NAKED RAVIOLI

Gnudi is the Italian word for nude. These delicious melt-in-your-mouth ricotta dumplings are actually the inside of a ravioli, but without the pasta clothing. You can use fresh ricotta found at Italian specialty stores or ricotta from the grocery refrigerator section.

Ingredients

15 oz. gluten-free ricotta cheese

1 large egg

⅓ cup Parmesan cheese

pinch of fresh nutmeg

salt and pepper to taste

½ cup Mary's Baking Mix

tapioca flour for dusting

Variations

Sun dried tomato gnudi: *Add ½ cup hydrated, minced sun dried tomatoes and ¼ cup toasted pine nuts. Eliminate nutmeg and add 2 TBL finely chopped basil. Add to dough after ricotta.*

Wild mushroom gnudi: *Sauté ½ cup wild mushrooms, such as shitake, crimini or porcini, with 2 TBL minced shallots, 1 TBL olive oil, salt and pepper. Eliminate nutmeg and add 2 TBL finely chopped sage. Add to dough after ricotta.*

MIX IT UP

☙ Line a colander with paper towels, and spoon in ricotta cheese. Let drain 30 minutes.

☙ In a medium bowl, beat egg, Parmesan cheese, nutmeg, salt and pepper.

☙ Mix in drained ricotta. Fold in Mary's Baking Mix, mixing gently until dough is combined. Refrigerate for at least 1 hour.

☙ Using two teaspoons or your hands, form a dough ball the size of a pecan and drop it into a small bowl of tapioca flour, dusting lightly. Add as little flour as possible to coat pasta. (In gluten-free pasta-making, a light hand with the flour makes for a more tender dough). Place on a parchment-lined baking sheet and repeat.

☙ Bring a large pot of salted water to boil. Cook 6–7 minutes. Gnudi will float to the top. Remove with a slotted spoon to a serving platter, and top with your favorite sauce, such as *Capone's Marinara Sauce, Brown Butter Sage Sauce, Alfredo Sauce,* or *Garlic and Olive Oil Sauce* (see pages 101, 94, or 110)

Makes 28 gnudi

DAIRY-FREE

Use *Mary's Dairy-Free Ricotta* (see page 113), and substitute ground toasted pine nuts or ground toasted walnuts for Parmesan cheese.

Gnocchi con Spinaci e Ricotta
SPINACH RICOTTA GNOCCHI

Making gnocchi was a favorite chore of mine as a child. Rolling the dough into little pear-shaped balls and dropping them into the bubbling water was as fun as eating them. Although traditionally made from potatoes, this recipe is a delicate version of an old classic. The light taste and fluffy consistency of this gnocchi will leave your guests begging for more.

MIX IT UP

PREHEAT OVEN TO 350 DEGREES. LIGHTLY GREASE A 9x13" BAKING DISH WITH BUTTER OR OIL.

Combine spinach and shallots in a small skillet with butter. Sauté until moisture is evaporated. Stir frequently until the mixture is dry and almost sticks to the pan. Pulse in a food processor or blender, or cut fine with a knife.

In a large bowl, add ricotta cheese, Parmesan cheese, egg yolks, tapioca flour, potato starch, nutmeg, salt and pepper. Add spinach puree to bowl and mix until combined. Refrigerate for ½ hour.

Using two teaspoons or with your hands, shape dough into pasta the size of a pecan. Dough will be soft and sticky. If mixture will not hold together, add tapioca flour, 1 tsp at a time, until you can work with the dough. Drop gnocchi into a bowl of white rice flour. Roll in flour, dusting off excess. Place on a parchment-lined baking sheet.

Drop gnocchi into a 6 quart pot of rapidly simmering (not boiling) water. Allow them to cook for 10 minutes, stirring gently once or twice to make sure they don't stick to each other. Remove with a slotted spoon.

Place gnocchi in a baking dish prepared with 2 TBL melted butter brushed evenly over bottom of the pan. Arrange gnocchi in a single layer. Add either tomato sauce or a sauce of melted butter and Parmesan cheese. Bake for 15 minutes.

Makes 30 gnocchi

Ingredients

½ lb. baby spinach leaves

2 TBL minced shallots

2–3 TBL unsalted butter, plus additional 2 TBL

1 cup gluten-free ricotta, well drained

⅓ cup Parmesan cheese

3 large egg yolks, beaten

¼ cup tapioca flour

3 TBL potato starch

pinch of freshly ground nutmeg

salt and pepper taste

white rice flour for dusting

DAIRY-FREE

Substitute *Mary's Dairy-Free Ricotta* (see page 113) for ricotta, and add ¼ cup toasted and finely chopped pine nuts or walnuts. Eliminate butter sauce, and top with a tomato sauce.

Gnocchi di Patata

POTATO GNOCCHI

Potato gnocchi is another delicious and easy to make pasta. I remember sitting in Aunt Carmel's kitchen watching with fascination as she easily rolled the dough into long, sausage-like shapes and then quickly finished each dumpling over the back of spiny fork. When I finally tried to make them I realized there are no secrets here. They are quite easy to make.

Ingredients

1½ lbs. baking potatoes (about 4 medium potatoes)

¾ cup Mary's Baking Mix

1 egg

¾ tsp salt

1/4 tsp grated nutmeg

Chef's Notes

Potatoes vary in size and depending upon what kind you use, you could end up with more than 1½ lbs. If your dough is too sticky to handle, add a little more Mary's Baking Mix. The dough should feel a little bit like thick mash potatoes. Idaho baking potatoes are good, but sometimes I like to use red potatoes for their sweet flavor.

MIX IT UP

✎ In a large pan, boil potatoes with skin on until they are easily pierced with a fork. Drain and peel.

✎ Put the potatoes through a food mill, or grate them on the large side of a cheese grater onto a wooden board or clean work surface.

✎ Add Mary's Baking Mix, salt, and nutmeg. Mix with potatoes, forming a mound with a well in the center.

✎ Break egg in the center and add salt. Knead dough until well incorporated. Dough should be smooth and fairly easy to handle. If dough is too sticky, dust your board lightly with Mary's Baking Mix. Only add enough Mary's Baking Mix to be able to handle the dough. Too much flour will make your gnocchi tough.

✎ Divide dough into 4 parts. On a Mary's Baking Mix-dusted work surface, roll each part into a long, sausage-like shape, about 1½" in diameter. With a knife cut each part into individual dumplings about 1" each.

✎ Set a fork face down on the end of your board, and dust it with Mary's Baking Mix. Gently roll each of your gnocchi over the back of the fork prongs.

✎ Bring a large pot of salted water to boil. Drop in a few gnocchi at a time, only enough to fill the bottom of the pot in a single layer. Gnocchi will soon rise to the surface of the water. Cook for additional 2–3 minutes. Remove gnocchi with a slotted spoon to a platter.

✎ Cover with your favorite sauce and sprinkle with Parmesan cheese if desired. Serve immediately.

Serves 6

Salsa Marinara

CAPONE'S MARINARA SAUCE

This recipe has been in my family for generations. In my grandfathers' day, they harvested their tomatoes from yard-sized gardens, blanched them (removing the skin and seeds) and diced them fine to create this basis sauce. Today, with the help of my brother Mark's recipe, I have substituted good whole tomatoes from a can to achieve a wonderful and very similar flavor. Making a great marinara sauce is an essential base for all tomato sauces. Many variations can happen from there.

MIX IT UP

❧ Run tomatoes through a food mill to remove skin and seeds, or push by hand through a colander, into a 6-quart sauce pan. Discard the tomato pulp left in the food mill or colander.

❧ Warm tomatoes on medium heat, and add basil, oregano, sugar, salt and pepper. Bring to a slow simmer until bubbles appear, releasing the water from the tomatoes and creating a paste. Cook 20 minutes or until the tomato sauce resembles a thin oatmeal. Stir frequently and do not overcook. Taste and adjust seasoning accordingly, for example: add more herbs for more flavor, if it is too sweet add a pinch of salt and pepper, if it is too salty add a pinch of sugar.

❧ In a small pan, heat oil and add minced garlic. Cook until lightly brown or just beginning to color. Add the oil and garlic to your sauce and stir.

Makes 4–6 servings

Ingredients

2 28 oz. cans whole tomatoes in basil

2 TBL fresh basil, chopped

1 TBL fresh oregano, chopped

1 TBL sugar

¼ tsp or more salt, to taste

fresh ground pepper to taste

¼ cup olive oil

2 cloves garlic, minced

Brother Mark and niece Kristen

Chef's Notes

Removing the skin and seeds from the tomatoes will decrease the acidity of the sauce. Cooking the tomatoes first before adding the olive oil and garlic will release the water from the tomatoes, creating a tomato paste. To ensure a delicious Marinara, make sure you buy whole tomatoes rather than diced or purée.

Salsa Alla Bolognese

CAPONE'S BOLOGNESE SAUCE

This sauce, made with the simple addition of seasoned meat to the Capone's Marinara, is both rich and savory. I like to use Capone's Bolognese sauce in my lasagna, manicotti or cannelloni dishes. Leftover Bolognese makes a pizza topping.

Ingredients

2 28 oz. cans whole tomatoes in basil

2 TBL fresh basil chopped

1 TBL fresh oregano

1 TBL sugar

¼ tsp or more salt, to taste

fresh ground pepper to taste

¼ cup olive oil

2 cloves garlic, minced

½ lb. meat (ground veal, Italian pork sausage with casing removed, pork shoulder, ground beef, ground dark turkey, ground turkey sausage with casing removed, and/or ground lamb)

1 TBL fresh marjoram, chopped

Chef's Notes

My favorite meat for this dish is braised pork shoulder slowly simmered on top of the stove with salt, pepper and marjoram and broth that covers about half way up the meat. Cook for 1 hour or until meat is tender and ready to fall off the bone. Remove the meat from the bone and add it to the sauce. Cook together for 30 minutes.

MIX IT UP

✍ Run tomatoes through a food mill to remove skin and seeds, or push by hand through a colander, into a 6-quart sauce pan. Discard the tomato pulp left in the food mill or colander.

✍ Warm tomatoes on medium heat, and add basil, oregano, sugar, salt and pepper. Bring to a slow simmer until bubbles appear, releasing the water from the tomatoes and creating a paste. Cook 20 minutes or until the tomato sauce resembles a thin oatmeal. Stir frequently and do not overcook. Taste and adjust seasoning accordingly, for example: add herbs for more flavor, if it is too sweet add a pinch of salt and pepper, if it is too salty add 1 tsp sugar.

✍ In a small pan, heat oil and add garlic. Cook until lightly brown or just beginning to color, about 1 minute. Add the oil and garlic to sauce and stir.

✍ Simmer meat in a saucepan with a little oil to prevent meat from sticking. Season with salt, pepper and fresh marjoram, and stir. Add meat mixture to sauce. Cook over low heat until flavors are incorporated, about 15–30 minutes.

Makes enough for 1 lb. gluten-free pasta

Salsa Marinara con Astice

CAPONE'S MARINARA WITH LOBSTER

The word marinara literally means from the sea. My family makes this seafood sauce on Christmas Eve served with breaded smelts, linguini with clam sauce, and baked stuffed flounder. But you don't have to wait for Christmas for this incredible meal. Served over a bed of gluten-free pasta with a fresh green salad and focaccia, this sauce makes any day a special occasion.

MIX IT UP

☞ Remove the lobster meat from shell, and set aside both meat and shell.

☞ Run tomatoes through a food mill to remove skin and seeds, or push by hand through a colander, into a 6 quart sauce pan. Discard the tomato pulp left in the food mill or colander.

☞ Warm tomatoes on medium heat, and add basil, parsley, sugar, salt and pepper. Add the shell of the lobster to the sauce. Bring to a slow simmer until bubbles appear, releasing the water from the tomatoes and creating a paste. Allow the lobster shell to infuse its flavor in the sauce. Remove shell.

☞ Cook 20 minutes or until the tomato sauce resembles a thin oatmeal. Stir frequently, and do not overcook. Taste and adjust seasoning accordingly, for example: add herbs for more flavor, if it is too sweet add a pinch of salt and pepper, if it is too salty add a pinch of sugar. By this time, the lobster shell will have infused its flavor in the sauce. Remove shell.

☞ In a small sauté pan, add olive oil, butter, red pepper flakes and garlic. Sauté 2 minutes. Add lobster meat and simmer until light golden brown, about 3 minutes. Add brandy and reduce until evaporated about 1 minute. Add white wine and reduce by half, about 3–5 minutes.

☞ Add lobster sauté to tomato sauce and stir. Cook together for an additional 5 minutes until flavors are incorporated. Serve over pasta.

Makes enough for 1 lb. gluten-free pasta

Ingredients

1 lb. lobster meat, whole or tail only, chopped and shells reserved

2 28 oz. cans whole tomatoes

2 TBL fresh basil, chopped

2 TBL fresh Italian flat-leaf parsley, chopped

1 TBL sugar

½ tsp salt

fresh ground pepper to taste

2 TBL olive oil

2 TBL butter, ghee or butter alternative

¼ tsp red pepper flakes

2 cloves garlic, minced

¼ cup brandy

½ cup white wine

Salsa Alle Vongole
WHITE CLAM SAUCE

This sauce is another simple, rich combination of olive oil, garlic, herbs — and this time, clams. You can use fresh, small hard-shelled clams or to make is super easy use baby clams in the can. Either one will give you a delicious sauce that requires little more than a good appetite.

Ingredients

3 lbs. small hard-shelled clams such as Manila or Littleneck, scrubbed and rinsed (or 1 18 oz. can baby clams in water, drained)

¼ cup olive oil

4 TBL butter

5 cloves garlic, chopped

3 TBL fresh Italian flat-leaf parsley, chopped

pinch of salt

pepper to taste

½ cup dry white wine

4 oz. clam juice or homemade fish stock

1 lb. cooked gluten-free pasta such as linguini

chopped parsley for garnish

Tomato sauce variation

Add 1 lb. fresh chopped Roma tomatoes after browning the garlic, and reduce for 30 minutes before adding clams.

DAIRY-FREE

Substitute alternative butter for butter, or use a total of ½ cup olive oil and eliminate butter.

MIX IT UP

☙ If using fresh clams, soak them in a cold water for 1 hour before cooking, then scrub and rinse. Set aside.

☙ In a large skillet, add olive oil and butter. When butter is melted, add garlic, parsley, salt and pepper. Sauté until garlic is light brown, about 3 minutes.

☙ Add wine, fresh clams and clam juice and cover skillet. Simmer over medium low heat until clams open, about 10 minutes. (If using canned clams, add clams and clam juice along with wine, and simmer together uncovered about 10 minutes).

☙ Remove clams with a slotted spoon, discarding any that have not opened. Set aside. (If using canned clams, skip this step and leave clams in sauce).

☙ Toss sauce with cooked gluten-free pasta, and top with clams and a garnish chopped parsley.

Makes enough for a scant 1 lb. gluten-free pasta

ALFREDO SAUCE

This simple, yet rich Alfredo sauce is a family favorite. Surprisingly easy to make, the result is an elegant, velvety sauce with a hint of nutmeg and roasted pine nuts. Unfortunately, without a good hard cheese substitute such as Parmigiano Reggiano or Pecorino Romano, this is a total dairy affair. And dieters, beware. This sauce packs in all the cream, cheese and butter it can hold. That's what makes it so good!

MIX IT UP

➤ In a small saucepan, warm cream over medium heat, about 3–5 minutes. Add butter and stir, letting it melt into the cream, about 3 minutes.

➤ Lower heat and gradually add Parmesan cheese, nutmeg and pepper and stir continuously with a whisk until sauce is smooth and velvety.

➤ Separate egg yolk and beat in a small bowl. Temper the yolk by adding a little of the sauce to the beaten egg, warming it to the sauce's temperature. Here's where timing becomes important. It is imperative that you have the pasta cooked and ready to serve since once you add the egg yolk the sauce will emulsify and thicken within minutes. If the sauce is left on the stove for too long you may get a broken texture. If this happens, whisk in a little more warm cream into the sauce to re-emulsify.

➤ Add egg yolk to cream sauce, and whisk continuously until sauce thickens, about 2 minutes.

➤ Immediately top hot cooked pasta with sauce and toss. Sprinkle with toasted pine nuts and fresh parsley if desired, and serve.

Makes enough for 1 lb. gluten-free pasta

Ingredients

1 cup heavy cream or half-and-half

6 TBL unsalted butter, chopped

1 cup Parmesan cheese, finely grated

pinch of nutmeg

¼ tsp white pepper

1 egg yolk

¼ cup toasted pine nuts (optional)

fresh Italian flat-leaf parsley, chopped

Salsa ai Carciofi

LEMON ARTICHOKE SAUCE

A refreshing sauce, made with artichoke hearts and the bright tastes of lemon and herbs, is perfect with homemade pasta. Light and delicate, this sauce takes only minutes to prepare. For a more robust flavor, you might add a bit of red pepper flakes or a tablespoon of capers. I also like it just the way it is.

Ingredients

1 lemon, juiced

1 14 oz. can artichoke hearts, drained and quartered

⅓ cup olive oil

2 TBL butter

3 cloves garlic, chopped

½ cup dry white wine

2 TBL fresh Italian flat-leaf parsley, chopped

salt and pepper to taste

½ cup Parmesan cheese

pinch of red pepper flakes or 1 TBL capers (optional)

MIX IT UP

❧ In a small bowl, add lemon juice and artichokes. Let sit for 30 minutes, drain and set aside.

❧ Heat olive oil and butter, and add garlic. Cook for 1 minute. Add artichokes to oil. Cook artichokes until they are light golden brown, turning occasionally, about 12 minutes.

❧ Add wine and reduce by half, about 5 minutes. Add parsley, salt and pepper. Add red pepper flakes or capers if desired. Cover and simmer for 2–3 minutes.

❧ In the meantime, prepare up 1 lb. gluten-free pasta. Drain and toss with artichoke sauce and half the Parmesan cheese. Sprinkle remaining cheese over the top.

Makes enough for 1 lb. gluten-free pasta

DAIRY-FREE

This sauce is excellent without Parmesan cheese. The bright taste of the lemony artichokes give it plenty of flavor. Substitute ghee or butter alternative for butter.

Chef's Notes

Be careful not to let your artichoke hearts marinate for longer than 30 minutes, or the lemon juice will make your sauce too tangy. If making fresh pasta, I like the basil pasta variation for this sauce.

Salsa alla Norma

EGGPLANT, TOMATOES AND OLIVE SAUCE

Salsa Norma gets its name from the opera Norma, for which it was invented. This is a great late-summer sauce, when the tomatoes and eggplants are at their best, but don't hesitate to make it in the middle of winter. This nutritional collection of vegetables will feed you well.

MIX IT UP

Blanch tomatoes in rapidly boiling water, just until their skins crack. Remove from water and set in a strainer to cool. Peel outer layer of skin and dice.

Heat olive oil on medium high heat and add eggplant. Brown on all sides and then remove to paper towel-lined platter to drain.

Reduce heat to medium, and add more oil if necessary. Add onion and cook until translucent, about 3 minutes. Add garlic and cook, about 2 minutes. Add tomatoes, basil, parsley, olives, capers, salt and pepper and simmer until tomatoes have lost most of their liquid, about 20 minutes.

Transfer eggplant to tomato sauce, and cook together until flavors are blended, about 15 minutes.

Serve over your favorite gluten-free pasta. Garnish with Parmesan cheese if desired.

Makes enough for 1 lb. gluten-free pasta

Ingredients

2 lbs. plum tomatoes

olive oil for frying

1 large purple globe eggplant, chopped

1 yellow onion, chopped

2 cloves garlic, minced

¼ cup fresh basil, chopped

¼ cup fresh Italian flat-leaf parsley, chopped

2 cups olives, such as calamata or a mild green olive of your choice, chopped

¼ cup capers, drained

salt and pepper to taste

Parmesan cheese for garnish

I PRIMI

WHITE BEAN AND COUNTRY ITALIAN SAUSAGE BOLOGNESE

This hearty winter ragù is as easy to make as it is rewarding to eat. The addition of cannellini or white kidney beans makes this a traditional Tuscan dish. Great served over plain pasta, chestnut pasta, ravioli or even rice. For a vegetarian version, use butternut squash in place of sausage.

Ingredients

2 TBL olive oil

1 small onion, chopped

1 large carrot, chopped

2 stalks celery, chopped

½ lb. Italian sausage, such as pork, turkey or chicken Italian-flavored sausage

2 TBL fresh Italian flat-leaf parsley, chopped

1 TBL fresh oregano, chopped

1 can white cannellini or white kidney beans, drained (or 2 cups fresh beans, cooked)

1 28 oz. can whole tomatoes, drained and chopped, liquid reserved)

pinch of salt

¼ tsp red pepper flakes

1 tsp sugar

1 cup vegetable, chicken or beef broth

Vegetarian variation

Eliminate sausage and add 1½ cups butternut squash, peeled and cubed. Season with parsley and oregano.

MIX IT UP

In a large skillet, heat olive oil over medium heat until hot. Add onion; sauté until translucent, about 3 minutes. Add carrot and celery. Sauté for an additional 2 minutes.

Remove the sausage from its casing and add to vegetables, breaking up the sausage into small bite-size pieces. Add parsley and oregano. Cook for 5 minutes, stirring occasionally, until meat begins to brown.

Add the remaining ingredients: beans and chopped tomatoes with the reserved liquid, salt, red pepper flakes, sugar and vegetable broth. Simmer uncovered over medium heat for 20 minutes, stirring occasionally or until sauce reduces to the desired thickness. Salt and pepper to taste.

Remove from heat and serve.

Makes enough for 1 lb. gluten-free pasta

Salsa Alla Marcella

BRUNNA'S TOMATO AND CHILI PEPPER SAUCE

I first tasted this delightful sauce at the table of my friend, Brunna, in Parma, Italia. What I found different was the light use of the fiery peperoncino, or dried hot chili peppers. I like to make it in the summertime when I can get all the fresh ingredients I need to make the flavors really pop. This rich, buttery, slightly spicy sauce is especially good on delicate homemade pasta or gnocchi, or on top of baked fish.

MIX IT UP

❧ Blanch tomatoes in rapidly boiling water, just until the skins crack. Remove from water and set in a strainer to cool. Peel outer layer of skin and dice. If using canned tomatoes, pass them through a food mill or colander to remove skin and seeds.

❧ In a saucepan over medium heat, add tomatoes, salt, pepper and sugar. Bring to a slow simmer until bubbles appear, releasing the water from the tomatoes and creating a paste. (Do not overcook or sauce will become bitter.) Simmer, stirring occasionally for 20–25 minutes.

❧ In a separate sauce pan, add butter or butter alternative, basil and chili peppers. Cook over low heat until butter is flavored with peppers, about 5 minutes. Don't let the butter brown. Remove peppers, tasting the butter sauce to make sure they have transferred their spice to your liking, and add butter mixture to the tomato paste. Cook together to combine flavors, about 5 minutes.

Makes enough for 1 lb. gluten-free pasta

Ingredients

2½ lbs. fresh Roma tomatoes, blanched, skinned and diced (or 2 28 oz. cans whole tomatoes)

¼ tsp or more salt to taste

fresh ground pepper to taste

2 heaping tsp sugar

¼ cup butter, ghee or butter alternative

6–8 leaves fresh basil, torn

6 tiny dried red chili peppers

4 cloves garlic, peeled and smashed

Aglio e Olio

GARLIC AND OLIVE OIL SAUCE

This simple sauce of olive oil and garlic is a staple for most Italian kitchens. My Uncle Georgie couldn't live without eating this dish at least once a week. Quite flavorful, this sauce is packed with the "good" fats of olive oil and the antibacterial and antioxidant properties of garlic. And it tastes great with or without grated cheese.

Ingredients

6 cloves garlic, chopped

½ cup olive oil

½ tsp red pepper flakes (or 2 small red chilis, chopped)

pinch of salt

Parmesan or Pecorino Romano cheese, grated (optional)

Add to 1 lb. cooked gluten-free pasta

MIX IT UP

✍ Boil water and cook pasta until it is *al dente*, tender but firm.

✍ In a 6-quart saucepan, sauté garlic in oil. Add pepper flakes, a pinch of salt and cook until garlic is light golden brown, about 2 minutes. Do not let garlic overcook, or it will turn bitter. Add drained pasta and stir, coating pasta with sauce, about 2 minutes.

✍ Serve immediately with grated Parmesan or Pecorino Romano cheese if desired.

Makes enough for 1 lb. gluten-free pasta

CAPONE'S BÉCHAMEL SAUCE

This white sauce is a complement to vegetarian lasagna, cannelloni, fish, or chicken. Great by itself or combined with a layer of red sauce — one brings out the good flavor of the other.

MIX IT UP

◈ Melt butter in small saucepan. Whisk in tapioca flour and cook until it thickens and combines, about 2 minutes. Do not let mixture brown.

◈ Heat milk in another saucepan and add warm milk to your tapioca roux. Whisk until smooth.

◈ Add salt, pepper and nutmeg and warm over low heat just until sauce is thick enough to coat the back of a spoon.

◈ Ladle over fish, chicken, vegetables, lasagna, or cannelloni and serve immediately.

Makes 2 cups

Ingredients

2 TBL butter, ghee or butter alternative

2 TBL tapioca flour

2 cups milk (or unsweetened soy milk, almond milk or milk alternative)

½ tsp salt

¼ tsp white pepper

pinch of fresh nutmeg

Chef's Notes

If sauce is too thick, add more milk. If it is too thin, make additional roux (1 TBL butter to 1 TBL tapioca flour) and whisk in.

CREAMY WALNUT AND TRADITIONAL PESTOS

I like to make fresh pesto throughout the summer season when my basil garden is at its best. It can be whipped up quite easily in a food processor or a blender and is ready in minutes. Here I've included two of my favorite variations for this simple sauce.

Ingredients: Creamy walnut pesto

1 cup walnuts, chopped

¼ cup gluten-free bread crumbs

2 TBL Parmesan cheese

½ cup fresh basil, chopped

1 clove garlic, chopped

½ cup cream, heavy cream or half-and-half

¼ cup olive oil

salt and pepper to taste

Ingredients: Traditional pesto

½ cup pine nuts

½ cup Parmesan cheese

1 cup fresh basil

2 cloves garlic, chopped

¾ cup olive oil

sea salt and pepper to taste

MIX IT UP: CREAMY WALNUT PESTO

❧ In a large dry skillet, toast walnuts until light brown and aromatic, about 2–3 minutes. Remove from heat.

❧ In a food processor or blender, add walnuts, bread crumbs, Parmesan cheese, basil, garlic, cream, olive oil, salt and pepper. Blend until creamy, about 1 minute.

❧ Pour sauce into a small sauce pan and heat to serve.

MIX IT UP: TRADITIONAL PESTO

❧ In a large dry skillet, toast pine nuts until light brown and aromatic, about 2–3 minutes. Remove from heat.

❧ In food processor or blender, add pine nuts, Parmesan cheese, basil, garlic, olive oil and salt and pepper. Blend until smooth, about 1 minute.

❧ Pour sauce into a small sauce pan and heat to serve.

Makes enough for 1 lb. gluten-free pasta

DAIRY-FREE

Walnut pesto: Omit Parmesan cheese, and substitute soy creamer for cream. Salt to taste.

Traditional pesto: Omit Parmesan cheese, and increase pine nuts to ¾ cup. Salt to taste.

MARY'S TRADITIONAL AND DAIRY-FREE RICOTTA

Whenever we used ricotta cheese in our family recipes, we always flavored it first with a few special ingredients. I have created a dairy-free ricotta recipe that can be substituted tit-for-tat for the cow's milk variety.

MIX IT UP: TRADITIONAL RICOTTA

☙ Mix ingredients together in a small bowl until smooth.

MIX IT UP: DAIRY-FREE RICOTTA

☙ In food processor, add all ingredients. Blend until smooth.

☙ Salt and pepper to taste.

Makes 1½ cups

Ingredients: Traditional ricotta

1 cup ricotta cheese

¼ cup Parmesan cheese

2 TBL fresh Italian flat-leaf parsley, chopped

pinch of nutmeg

salt and pepper to taste

1 egg

Ingredients: Dairy-free ricotta

1 cup firm tofu

2 TBL toasted nuts such as walnuts, pine nuts, or sesame seeds

2 TBL gluten-free bread crumbs

2 TBL fresh Italian flat-leaf parsley, chopped

1 TBL fresh basil, chopped

1–2 cloves garlic, minced

pinch of nutmeg

salt and pepper to taste

1 egg

I Secondi

MAIN COURSE
MEATS, POULTRY, SEAFOOD, RISOTTO

Chicken and Country Vegetable Stew, 119

Chicken Cutlets In Lemon Sauce, 120

Herb Chicken with Blackberry Sauce, 121

Chicken with Prosciutto and Sage, 122

Parmesan Cheese Chicken, 123

Easy Oven Risotto, 124

Seafood Risotto, 125

Butternut Squash Risotto with Balsamic Vinegar Glaze, 126

Lobster Risotto, 127

Shrimp Scampi, 128

Sea Bass with Potato and Wild Mushroom Au Gratin, 129

Fried Seafood and Vegetable Platter, 130

Italian Omelet, 131

Cannelloni, 132

Manicotti, 133

Eggplant Parmesan, 134

Wild Mushroom and Vegetable Lasagna, 135

Mama Capone's Traditional Lasagna, 136

Pancetta, Arugula and Tomato Sandwich, 137

Braised Pork Loin with Apricot Gravy. 138

Sausage and Herb Polenta, 140

Sausage and Peppers, 141

Pizza Steak, 142

Poppie's Meatballs, 143

Stuffed Flank Steak, 144

Tuffy Levo's Braised Beef Ribs, 145

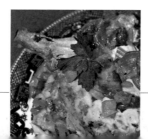

I Secondi

While in Italy dining with my American friend and her Italian husband, we began our meal with an antipasto of mussels, followed by a bowl of fresh pumpkin risotto and an *insalata mista*. I was feeling quite satisfied as I finished my glass of the *vino di casa*, when to my surprise my friend's husband asked, "What shall we take for dinner?"

In Italy, *il secondo*, or main course, represents the important center of the meal. Comprised of roasted, fried, broiled and braised meats topped with gravies and sauces or stuffed with a delectable stuffing, *il secondo* is often a reflection of the importance of the guests at the table.

In more recent years, this course has also included fish, and sometimes even the humble egg in a *frittata*. In any case, Italians take their *i secondi* seriously — and with good reason. The first time I traveled to Italy in 1985, I was struck by how fresh the memory of World War II was for the older generation. Meat dishes were very hard to come by during the war. In fact, I heard more than one story of families living on chestnuts for years with not a chicken in sight.

Although the art of the six-course meal has been somewhat forgotten by Italian-Americans, the importance of the main course has not. I still remember sitting at my grandfather's table swathed in a cloth napkin larger than my dress, devouring plates of chicken cacciatore, braciole, or braised pork loin covered in a rich ragu. My father often made use of bistecca, or beef steak, and created scrumptious dishes such as pizza steak and Roman stew. Since fish was once reserved for Friday "fasting," it became associated with religious holidays. Our Christmas Eve meal was, and still is, filled with trays of breaded seafood *fritto* platters, shrimp scampi, mussels in wine broth and fried breaded anchovies.

In this section, I have included complex pasta dishes like lasagna, manicotti and cannelloni. I have even included risottos since they can stand alone as a complete meal. Although these dishes are classified in Italy to be a first course, for the American diet I consider them a main course. There are also more traditional meat and fish dishes… a collection of my family's favorites.

All of these main course recipes are proportioned to make a full meal. If you'd like to eat more like the Italians, reduce the amounts on each plate and enjoy *il antipasto*, *il primo*, *il secondo* and *le verdure*. Just make sure to save room for *le dolce*, the dessert.

Choosing meats

❧ When choosing meats I look for both taste and quality. Free-range animals raised without hormones or antibiotics are superior. I often substitute bison or buffalo meat for beef, as bison is low in fat and high in protein and iron.

❧ Grass-fed beef is also a good alternative to conventionally raised beef, as it is higher in heart-healthy omega-3 fatty acids and lower in fat. In addition, grass-fed cattle are not raised in feedlots, where cattle can be subjected to pollutants.

❧ I recommend natural pork, raised without antibiotics or unnecessary preservatives. There are now a variety of natural pork sausages available at meat counters, as well as sausages made with free-range turkey, beef, buffalo and chicken.

❧ Choose fish by what is in season; your local grocer can help you decide. Fish is fresh if the skin and flesh are firm. Use the fish the day you buy it. If you are not using your fish for several days, sprinkle it lightly with coarse salt and freeze. Lobsters are trapped all year. I always buy live mussels and store them on ice until ready to clean and cook. There is some question about the pollutants circulated in farm-raised fish, so I prefer wild-caught fish whenever possible.

❧ I always recommend free-range, natural or organic chicken.

❧ With eggs, the choice is simple: free-range, organic eggs are an inexpensive ingredient to indulge in, one that is in many of my recipes.

The art of risotto-making

Risotto is another of the great gifts Italy has given to the world, especially to gluten-free dieters. Simple medium-grain rice is dressed up with seasonal ingredients, rich broths, meat and fish, bringing out extraordinary flavor combinations. Although risotto is traditionally thought of as a *primo piatto*, or first course, I'm including it in this main course section because I consider it a full meal. A beautiful risotto dish takes a little time and some simple technique to get it right. But once you master the technique, you can let your imagination run wild.

❧ Choose a *superfino* (superfine) or *fino* (fine) medium-grain rice grown in Northern Italy. Arborio is the most commonly used rice, and is readily available in any store. Arborio has a slightly nutty taste and is a starchy medium-grain rice that absorbs more liquid than long-grain rice. Other good varieties are Carnaroli, Balso, Roma, Martatelli or fine Vialone. Whichever rice you choose, rinse it thoroughly until the water runs clear.

❧ Making risotto demands your full attention. Risotto usually requires 20–25 minutes of almost constant stirring until all the liquid has been added and absorbed. At the beginning, I like to stir a little less. Permitting a minute or two to pass between strokes will allow the rice to absorb the liquid between ladles.

❧ Use a large, heavy-bottomed stock pot or a 10" saucepan to carry heat evenly and to prevent scorching. The pot needs to be large enough to hold the rice, giving you room to stir as the rice expands to three times it original size. Avoid using a skillet since liquid will evaporate too quickly.

❦ Stock must be simmering and warm when added to the rice. Cold stock will lower the temperature of the pot and stop the rice from absorbing liquid properly, causing a starchy mess.

❦ After initially cooking rice until it turns a pearly white (about 2–3 minutes), add 1 cup of hot broth mixture. Simmer and stir frequently until rice has absorbed broth, about 4 minutes. Repeat this process until broth is absorbed or until risotto is done. The amount of broth used varies from recipe to recipe and is dependent upon the rice you use.

❦ Here's where the art comes in. Taste your risotto periodically to test for doneness. Your final results should be moist and creamy but not pudding-like. *Al dente* is the proper Italian term, meaning slightly firm, yet tender. If your rice is done before you have used up the broth, do not add the rest just because it's there. If your rice is too firm and you need more broth, add a little at a time. If you run out of broth, use hot water.

❦ Substitute wine for broth, or for that matter, broth for wine if you are eliminating the wine from the recipe.

❦ If adding Parmesan cheese, add it before the last ladle of broth. Do not use Parmesan cheese with seafood risotto. Italians feel that it spoils the fresh taste of the fish.

❦ If you have seen the movie "The Big Night" you know how important it is to serve risotto immediately. I have the table set and my family sitting at it about 5 minutes before I anticipate the risotto being done. For the perfect tasting of this well-earned dish, serve *pronto*!

Pollo alla Cacciatora

CHICKEN AND COUNTRY VEGETABLE STEW

My grandfather, Tuffy Levo, made cacciatore every Friday, which he called "junk." At the end of the week he would empty his refrigerator, combining different leftover meats and vegetables in a tasty ragu sauce. This variation of junk uses fresh ingredients, adding a pinch of this and a little of that, much in his tradition. Feel free to create your own unique junk.

MIX IT UP

❧ Place chicken thighs skin down on a cutting board and cut thigh meat in two lengthwise, leaving the bone attached to one side and the skin on. Salt and pepper meat and add to a large skillet with heated olive oil. Sauté for 5 minutes over medium-high heat until brown. Remove to a large bowl, including juices.

❧ Add sausage to the pan and sauté until brown, about 5 minutes. Remove to bowl with chicken.

❧ Add more oil if necessary and sauté onion until translucent, about 5 minutes. Add carrots and green beans, and simmer another 5 minutes, scraping and incorporating meat drippings from the bottom of the pan.

❧ Stir in marjoram, parsley, garlic, lemon peel and red pepper flakes. Cook for 3 minutes, combining flavors.

❧ Add wine and reduce by half, boiling for 3–5 minutes. Stir in tomatoes with juice and chicken or vegetable broth and bring to a boil.

❧ Add meat to pan and reduce to simmer. Cook covered for 30 minutes.

❧ With a slotted spoon, remove chicken and sausage to bowl and reduce sauce. Uncovered, simmer for 20 minutes. Salt and pepper to taste.

❧ Return meat to sauce and heat together. Serve with grated Parmesan or Pecorino Romano cheese over gluten-free pasta or rice.

Serves 6

Ingredients

6–8 chicken thighs, with skin and bones

2 TBL olive oil

1 lb. sausage such as Italian pork, turkey or chicken, cut into 1" pieces

1 large yellow onion, chopped

2 medium carrots, chopped

1 cup flat Italian green beans, chopped into 1" pieces

½ cup fresh marjoram, chopped

¼ cup fresh Italian flat-leaf parsley, chopped

5 cloves garlic, minced

1 tsp grated lemon peel

½ tsp red pepper flakes

1 cup dry red wine

1 28 oz. can whole tomatoes in juice, chopped

2 cups vegetable or chicken broth

salt and pepper to taste

Chef's Notes

A good, basic ragu includes diced onions and carrots. Sometimes I like to add peas, mushrooms, peppers or even sweet potatoes.

Scaloppine di Pollo

CHICKEN CUTLETS IN LEMON SAUCE

This dish can be made with chicken, veal or even turkey breast. The trick is to pound out the meat thin and create a crisp crust before adding the bright lemon sauce.

Ingredients

6 boneless, skinless chicken breasts, turkey breasts or veal cutlets

olive oil for frying

3 TBL tapioca flour

2 egg yolks, beaten

1 cup gluten-free bread crumbs

½ lemon, juiced

½ cup white wine

3 TBL capers (optional)

2 TBL fresh Italian flat-leaf parsley

salt and pepper to taste

MIX IT UP

With a meat tenderizer or mallet, pound out the chicken breasts between two pieces of plastic wrap until meat is very thin, about ½". Pat dry with paper towels and salt and pepper both sides.

In a large skillet, heat olive oil over medium heat.

Dip chicken breasts in tapioca flour, egg yolks and then bread crumbs; add to hot olive oil. Fry until chicken beasts are golden brown and crispy, about 5 minutes per side. Add more olive oil if needed to keep them from sticking.

Add lemon juice, wine, capers and parsley. Simmer, reducing sauce by half, about 10 minutes.

Remove from heat. Serve with sauce over rice or gluten-free pasta.

Serves 6

HERB CHICKEN WITH BLACKBERRY SAUCE

Slow-roasted, savory meat is one of my favorite cold-weather foods. My family goes crazy over this easy-to-prepare dish with its rich, savory flavors and delicious blackberry-herb reduction. You can substitute Cornish game hens, turkey, lamb or beef as the meat in this dish.

MIX IT UP: CHICKEN

PREHEAT OVEN TO 425 DEGREES.

➤ Add to blender or food processor: butter, thyme, lemon juice, lemon zest and garlic. Blend until creamy and well incorporated.

➤ Carefully lift skin from the chicken, and smear the butter mixture between the meat and the skin. Add salt and pepper to the outside of the meat.

➤ Place chicken on a roasting pan with a tightly fitting rack, breast side down.

➤ Roast 15 minutes at 425 degrees to seal in juices, and then lower oven temperature to 350 degrees. Cook until chicken breast is firm to the touch. Bake about 15 more minutes, or until internal temperature reaches 150 degrees.

MIX IT UP: BLACKBERRY SAUCE

➤ Heat oil in a medium saucepan over medium heat, and sauté shallots and thyme until shallots are translucent, about 3 minutes. Add garlic. Sauté for 2 minutes.

➤ Add wine, and simmer until reduced by one-third, about 5 minutes. Add blackberries and broth, and bring to a gentle boil, reducing again until one-third of the liquid is gone, about 10 minutes. Salt and pepper to taste.

➤ Strain sauce, squeezing juice from berries. Discard pulp.

➤ Transfer chicken breasts to a plate, and drizzle with the blackberry reduction sauce.

Serves 6

Ingredients: Chicken

6 TBL unsalted butter, ghee or butter alternative

1 TBL fresh thyme, minced

2 tsp fresh-squeezed lemon juice

zest of ½ lemon

1 clove garlic, minced

6 chicken breasts, with skin and bones

salt and pepper to taste

Ingredients: Blackberry sauce

1 TBL olive oil

½ cup shallots, chopped

2 tsp garlic, minced

2 TBL fresh thyme, stemmed and chopped

1 cup port wine

2 cups fresh or frozen blackberries, thawed

1 cup vegetable or chicken broth

salt and pepper to taste

Meat variations

If you are roasting lamb chops or beef, rub the compound butter on the outside of the meat, sear on medium high heat in skillet until brown, and then roast in the oven to desired temperature.

Saltimbocca di Pollo

CHICKEN WITH PROSCIUTTO AND SAGE

This classic Roman dish literally means chicken that "jumps in your mouth." Made with tapioca flour as breading, these tasty chicken breasts with a white wine sauce will disappear before your eyes.

Ingredients

4 small boneless, skinless chicken breasts

5 TBL unsalted butter, divided

½ cup tapioca flour

½ cup Asiago cheese, finely grated

8 thin slices prosciutto

⅔ cup dry white wine

2 TBL fresh sage, minced

2 TBL butter, ghee or butter alternative

whole fresh sage leaves for garnish

DAIRY-FREE

Omit Asiago cheese, and substitute ¼ cup of lightly toasted and salted sesame seeds for topping.

MIX IT UP

PREHEAT OVEN TO 375 DEGREES. LINE A BAKING DISH WITH PARCHMENT PAPER.

≈ Pound chicken breasts to ¼" thick. In a large skillet, melt 3 TBL of the butter over medium high heat. Dust chicken breasts with tapioca flour, and salt and pepper to taste. Sauté chicken breasts until brown, turning over once, about 5 minutes.

≈ Remove skillet from heat. Place cooked chicken breasts in the lined baking dish. Top each with 2 TBL Asiago cheese and 2 slices prosciutto. Place in oven and bake for 5 minutes until chicken is cooked through.

≈ Return skillet to the heat. Add wine, sage and the remaining 2 TBL butter. Whisk brown butter scrapings from bottom of the pan. Bring to a boil. Reduce until sauce is ⅓ cup, about 5 minutes.

≈ Transfer chicken to a platter. Garnish with sage leaves, and drizzle with pan butter sauce.

Serves 4

Pollo con Formaggio
PARMESAN CHEESE CHICKEN

My father made this chicken dish on top of the stove in his favorite skillet. I like using a hot oven, which makes this delicious dish a 20-minute affair. The secret ingredients are the mayonnaise and fresh herbs.

MIX IT UP

PREHEAT OVEN TO 450 DEGREES. LINE A BAKING SHEET WITH PARCHMENT PAPER.

🍃 Pound meat with a meat tenderizer until cutlets are tenderized and about ½" thick.

🍃 Combine gluten-free bread crumbs and cheese on a plate.

🍃 Combine mayonnaise and herbs in a small bowl.

🍃 Brush a quarter of the mayonnaise mixture on both sides of the cutlets, and then firmly press them onto the bread crumb plate, coating both sides. Place on the baking sheet. Sprinkle the cutlets with black pepper.

🍃 Place in oven and cook for 20 minutes or until chicken is firm to touch.

Serves 4

Ingredients

4 boneless, skinless chicken breasts

1 cup gluten-free bread crumbs

1 cup Parmesan cheese, shredded

¼ cup mayonnaise

3 TBL fresh herbs such as Italian flat-leaf parsley, basil, oregano or a combination, finely chopped

pepper to taste

EASY OVEN RISOTTO

Risotto is a lovely creamy rice dish that, with a few additions such as fresh vegetables, meat or seafood, can easily make a one-dish meal. This oven recipe makes this dish a snap.

Ingredients

3½ cups vegetable or chicken stock

3 TBL olive oil

1 TBL butter, ghee or butter alternative

1 large yellow onion, diced

2 cloves garlic, minced

½ lb. mushrooms such as baby portabella, crimini or shitake, stemmed and sliced

1½ tsp salt

2 TBL fresh herbs such as basil, Italian flat-leaf parsley or marjoram

1½ cups Arborio rice, rinsed thoroughly

1 cup baby peas

½ cup grated Parmesan cheese

pepper to taste

DAIRY-FREE

Omit Parmesan cheese, and add more salt and pepper to taste. Decrease your stock by ¼–½ cup. Stock amounts will depend on the type of rice you use and the ingredients you add, so experiment. A little less in this dish is better than a little more.

MIX IT UP

PREHEAT OVEN TO 350 DEGREES. SET OUT A 9x13" BAKING DISH.

≫ In a medium saucepan, heat stock to a boil; then lower the temperature to simmer while preparing risotto.

≫ In a large saucepan, warm oil and butter over medium high heat. Add onion. Sauté about 3 minutes. Add garlic; cook for an additional minute.

≫ Add mushrooms, salt, pepper and herbs. Sauté for 3 minutes.

≫ Lower heat. Add rice; stir and coat with oil. Cook until the grain begins to turn a pearly white, about 2–3 minutes.

≫ Gradually stir all of the hot stock into the rice pot. Add peas, and simmer for an additional 2 minutes.

≫ Pour rice mixture into a casserole dish, and cover with lid or foil. Bake 20 minutes or until rice is almost tender. Remove cover, and stir in the Parmesan cheese. Bake for another 10 minutes or until all liquid is absorbed and rice is tender.

Serves 4–6

SEAFOOD RISOTTO

This seafood risotto combines the simple grain of Arborio rice with the delicate flavors of the sea. I like to use a light stock with this dish and then brighten it up with lemon juice, which replaces any need for cheese.

MIX IT UP

In a large skillet, heat 1 TBL of the olive oil and 1 TBL of the butter over medium high heat. Add shrimp and scallops. Sauté for about 2 minutes, just until shrimp turns pink and scallops are lightly browned. Add wine, salt, pepper, 2 TBL of the lemon juice and garlic, and reduce until liquid is absorbed, about 3 minutes. Remove and transfer to a platter.

In a medium saucepan, heat stock over low heat. Depending on which stock you use (commercial stock may have enough salt, whereas homemade stock might need more), you may want to add a teaspoon of salt. Keep it warm but not boiling.

In a large saucepan, heat remaining 1 TBL olive oil over medium high heat. Add onion and parsley, and cook until soft and translucent, about 3 minutes. Add rice; stir and coat with oil. Cook until the grain begins to turn pearly white, about 2–3 minutes.

Add 1 cup of hot stock to rice mixture. Simmer, stirring frequently until rice has absorbed broth, about 4 minutes. Continue adding the remaining broth a ladle-full at a time. Stir frequently, adding more liquid as the rice absorbs each addition. Risotto is done when it is *al dente*, or firm but tender. This should take 20–25 minutes. If your rice is done before you have used up the broth, do not add the rest. If your rice is too firm and you need more broth, add a little at a time. If you run out of broth, use hot water.

Remove pan from heat, and stir in the remaining lemon juice (to taste) and salt and pepper.

Divide risotto between dinner plates. Top each plate with equal amounts of shrimp and scallops. Garnish each plate with a wedge of lemon.

Serves 4–6

Ingredients

2 TBL olive oil, divided

2 TBL butter, ghee or butter alternative, divided

½ lb. jumbo shrimp, shelled and de-veined

½ lb. large sea scallops

½ cup dry white wine

juice of 1 lemon, divided

1 clove garlic, chopped

5 cups stock such as fish, chicken or vegetable

1 sweet onion such as Vidalia, chopped

1 TBL fresh Italian flat-leaf parsley, chopped

1 ½ cups Arborio rice, rinsed thoroughly

salt and pepper to taste

lemon wedges for garnish

Chef's Notes

In Italy, combining seafood with cheese is a definite no-no. Italians believe that cheese takes away from the fresh taste of seafood. Instead, you can enhance your seafood dishes with a squeeze of lemon and/or a dash of salt.

BUTTERNUT SQUASH RISOTTO WITH BALSAMIC VINEGAR GLAZE

There are so many ways to make this versatile grain. Here's another of my favorites. This dish can be served along with a meat entrée or as a main course with a fresh green salad.

Ingredients

1 small butternut squash (about 1 lb.)

4–5 cups vegetable or chicken stock

¼ cup sherry

2 TBL olive oil

1 small yellow onion, diced

1 tsp fresh thyme, stemmed and chopped

1 TBL fresh Italian flat-leaf parsley, chopped

1 cup water

1½ cups Arborio rice, rinsed thoroughly

½ cup Parmesan cheese, finely grated

¼ cup balsamic vinegar

1 TBL brown sugar

1 tsp or more salt

2 TBL butter, ghee or butter alternative

pepper to taste

DAIRY-FREE

Omit Parmesan cheese and sprinkle top with toasted sesame seeds. Salt to taste.

MIX IT UP

☙ Trim stem, peel and cut squash in half lengthwise. Scoop out seeds and fibrous center. Quarter each half, and then slice each piece into thin, ⅛" slices.

☙ Heat stock and sherry in a small saucepan over low heat. Depending on the stock you use (commercial stock may have enough salt, whereas homemade stock might need more), add 1 tsp salt. Keep warm.

☙ In a large saucepan, heat olive oil over medium high heat, and add onion. Cook until soft and translucent, about 3 minutes. Add squash, thyme and parsley, and cover with about 1 scant cup water. Simmer uncovered over medium low heat until squash is soft and tender, about 15 minutes.

☙ Add rice and 1 cup of the hot broth mixture to the vegetable pot. Simmer, stirring frequently until rice has absorbed broth, about 4 minutes. Add another cup of broth and repeat, stirring until broth is absorbed. If your rice is done before you have used up the broth, do not add the rest. If your rice is too firm and you need more broth, add a little at a time. If you run out of broth, use hot water. This should take 20–25 minutes.

☙ Add Parmesan cheese before you add the last of the broth, and incorporate into rice mixture. Continue adding broth until rice is *al dente*, or firm but tender.

☙ In a small saucepan, add balsamic vinegar and brown sugar. Bring to a light boil, and whisk frequently. Sauce will begin to thicken and resemble a syrup, thick enough to coat the back of a spoon, about 5 minutes. Remove from stove and keep warm.

☙ When rice is ready, remove risotto pan from heat, and adjust salt and pepper. Stir in butter. Divide portions among plates, and drizzle with warm balsamic vinegar glaze. Serve immediately.

Serves 4–6

Risotto con Astice

LOBSTER RISOTTO

A little lobster goes a long way in this delicious version of risotto. One lobster tail makes both the broth and the meat for this savory dish. Add some saffron and a can of whole tomatoes, and the final result is exquisite.

MIX IT UP

Prepare *Fish Stock*, substituting the lobster shell for fish bones or fillet. Or add the lobster shell to *Vegetable Stock* or *Chicken Stock,* and simmer for 30 minutes before using. This will infuse the flavor of the lobster into the stock. Keep stock warm over low heat.

In a large saucepan, heat olive oil over medium heat, and add onion. Cook until soft and translucent, about 3 minutes. Add garlic; cook for an additional minute. Add lobster meat and parsley. Sauté until meat begins to cook, about 2 minutes.

Add rice. Stir and coat with oil, and cook until the grain begins to turn a pearly white, about 2–3 minutes. Combine saffron threads with 1 cup of stock. Add to rice, stirring until liquid is absorbed. Stir in chopped tomatoes, reserving juice for another recipe.

Continue adding the remaining broth one ladle-full at a time. Stir frequently, adding more liquid as the rice absorbs each addition. Risotto is done when it is *al dente*, or firm but tender. This process should take 20–25 minutes. If your rice is done before you have used up the broth, do not add the rest. If your rice is too firm and you need more broth, add a little at a time. If you run out of broth, use hot water.

Remove risotto from heat, and add butter, salt and pepper. Serve immediately.

Serves 6

Ingredients

½ lb. lobster tail, chopped, shell reserved

4–5 cups Fish, Chicken or Vegetable Stock (see pages 42—44)

2 TBL olive oil

1 small yellow onion, diced

1 clove garlic, minced

1 TBL fresh Italian flat-leaf parsley, chopped

1 ½ cups Arborio rice, rinsed thoroughly

½ tsp dried saffron threads, crushed

1 14 oz. can whole tomatoes, chopped and juice reserved

1 tsp or more salt

2 TBL butter, ghee or butter alternative

pepper to taste

Chef's Notes

A ½ lb. lobster tail is affordable enough to make this dish an mid-week meal. For special occasions, 2 lobster tails make a deliciously decadent dish.

Gamberi con Alio e Olio

SHRIMP SCAMPI

The secret to great shrimp scampi is the abundant use of fresh garlic. I started out making this recipe with three cloves of minced garlic and then just kept adding more. And why not! Garlic is one of the healthiest foods on the planet, full of antiviral and anti-carcinogen properties. And it tastes great. Makes enough for a scant one pound pasta or rice.

Ingredients

½ cup olive oil

4 TBL butter, ghee or butter alternative

1 small onion, diced

5–6 cloves garlic, chopped

1 lb. medium shrimp (31–40), peeled and deveined

½ cup white wine

3 TBL fresh Italian flat–leaf parsley, chopped

1 cup grape or cherry tomatoes, cut in half

½ lemon, juiced

½ tsp salt

fresh ground pepper to taste

fresh Italian flat-leaf parsley, chopped and/or red pepper flakes for garnish

About ¾ lb. gluten-free pasta such as spaghetti, linguini or fettuccine

MIX IT UP

 Heat olive oil and butter in a large skillet over medium heat. Add onion; cook for 3 minutes. Add garlic; cook for 2 minutes. Add shrimp, and cook for 2–3 minutes or until shrimp turn pink.

 Add wine, parsley, tomatoes and lemon juice; reduce liquids by half. Simmer about 15 minutes. Salt and pepper to taste.

 Cook gluten-free pasta. Drain, rinse and add back into the pot with the sauce, saving about ½ cup for the top. Toss and warm over low heat for 2–3 minutes until pasta is coated. If using rice, transfer rice to a platter and ladle sauce over top.

 Garnish with fresh parsley and/or red pepper flakes.

Serves 4–6

Tortellini in Brodo, 97; Antipasto Martini, 26; Cousin Maria, Pontelatone Italy; Mary's Antipasto, 27

Pesce con patate e funghi

SEA BASS WITH POTATO AND WILD MUSHROOM AU GRATIN

I love making baked, wrapped fish dishes. This one is a simple casserole of vegetables, potatoes and the fresh fish of the day with an olive oil-herb marinade. The recipe calls for thick fillets of sea bass. You can substitute monkfish, halibut steak or a white fish of your choice.

MIX IT UP

PREHEAT OVEN TO 350 DEGREES. LIGHTLY SPRAY A 9x9" OR LARGER CASSEROLE DISH.

🍃 Melt butter in a sauté pan over medium heat, add mushrooms and sauté until they begin to brown, about 5 minutes. Sprinkle with sea salt and pepper. Add brandy and reduce by half. Cook for about 3 minutes.

🍃 Mix together olive oil, rosemary, garlic, salt and pepper.

🍃 Arrange half of the potatoes on the bottom of the casserole dish. Drizzle with half of the olive oil mixture. Add half of the mushrooms and layer the remaining potatoes on top. Drizzle with remaining olive oil mixture. Add remaining mushrooms.

🍃 Wash and dry fish fillet(s), and lightly salt and pepper. Wrap the prosciutto around the fish, and lay on top of mushrooms. Add ¼ cup lemon juice over the top. Sprinkle with lemon zest.

🍃 Pour cream over casserole and cover with foil. Bake 45 minutes or until potatoes are tender. Bake uncovered for an additional 15 minutes, or until potatoes are done. Serve with a wedge of lemon.

Serves 4

Ingredients

4 TBL butter, ghee or butter alternative

½ lb. wild mushrooms such as shitake, crimini or oyster, sliced

½ tsp sea salt

2 TBL brandy (optional)

¼ cup olive oil

3 sprigs fresh rosemary, stemmed and chopped

3 cloves garlic, minced

2 lbs. yellow Yukon or russet potatoes, washed and sliced ⅛" thick

1½ lbs. thick, mild white fish such as sea bass, monkfish, halibut or whitefish

3–4 very thin slices prosciutto

¼ cup fresh lemon juice (about 1 lemon, squeezed)

1 TBL lemon zest

1 cup cream, such as heavy, half-and-half or unsweetened milk alternative (optional)

pepper to taste

lemon wedges for garnish

I SECONDI

Fritto di Pesce e Verdure

FRIED SEAFOOD AND VEGETABLE PLATTER

When I was visiting my friend in Northern Italy, we dined at a restaurant that was famous for their fritto di pesce e verdure, or fried fish and vegetable platter. Friends joined us, and we sat around a large table that was topped with a huge platter of delicately battered shrimp and vegetables along with a light garlic mayonnaise. The more we ate from this giant antipasto, the more the platter seemed to fill up. I have made a gluten-free tempura and sauces to emulate this fine dish, and although it is considered in Italy to be an antipasto, I serve it as a main course.

Ingredients

2 large eggs

1 cup white rice flour

½ cup tapioca flour

1 cup water

2 ice cubes

1 medium zucchini, cut into matchsticks

1 medium onion, cut into straws

10 stalks asparagus, cleaned and trimmed

1 yellow or red pepper, thinly sliced

½ lb. shrimp (31–40), peeled and deveined

½ lb. bay scallops

lemon peel from 1 large lemon, peeled in thin strips

6 figs, cut in half

canola or coconut oil for frying

chopped fresh Italian flat-leaf parsley and lemon wedges as garnish

¼ cup mayonnaise

1–2 cloves garlic, minced

¼ tsp lemon juice

salt and pepper to taste

MIX IT UP

LINE A BAKING SHEET WITH PAPER TOWELS.

In a small bowl, mix together eggs, rice flour, tapioca flour, water, salt and pepper. Add ice cubes, and set aside for 30 minutes.

Prepare zucchini, onion, asparagus, pepper, lemon peel and figs; clean shrimp and scallops.

In a large saucepan or deep skillet, heat 2" oil until it is smoking slightly. Oil temperature should reach 350 degrees. Dip vegetables in tempura batter. Add to oil in small batches. Do not overcrowd your pan.

Cook for 2–3 minutes until deep, golden brown. Place on a lined baking tray, and sprinkle with sea salt. Place in a warm oven. Repeat until all fish and vegetables are cooked.

Transfer to a large platter. Garnish with lemon slices and parsley. Mix together dip of mayonnaise, garlic and lemon juice. Salt and pepper to taste. Serve immediately.

Serves 6

Frittata

ITALIAN OMELET

My mother waits for spring when fresh, tender asparagus begins to appear in the marketplace. It's her favorite time to make frittata, the Italians' answer to the French omelet. Easy to make, this humble yet healthy dish is often served as a main course.

MIX IT UP

❧ Stem asparagus spears until they are *al dente,* or tender but firm.

❧ Beat eggs, chives, Pecorino Romano cheese, salt and pepper until blended. Add olive oil to a 10" crepe pan or non-stick skillet and heat over medium heat. When olive oil is hot, pour in egg mixture, swirling it to the edges of the pan. Add asparagus spears with ends in the middle and tips fanning out to the edges. Continue to agitate the pan, swirling eggs and moving loose egg mixture to the edges to cook.

❧ When the bottom is set and the top is resembles soft scrambled eggs, place a large plate over the top of the pan and flip the frittata onto it. Slide the uncooked side of frittata back into pan and cook until set, about 3 minutes. Center should still be soft. Slide onto warm plate to help inflate the frittata while serving.

❧ Garnish with a sprinkle Pecorino Romano if desired.

Makes one 10" frittata

Ingredients

8–10 fresh asparagus spears, washed, trimmed and steamed

6 large eggs

1 TBL fresh chives, chopped

2 TBL Pecorino Romano, finely grated (optional)

1½ TBL olive oil or ghee

salt and pepper to taste

Pancetta and zucchini frittata: *Add 4 slices pancetta to pan and cook over low heat until well done. Remove from pan and crumble. Slice zucchini thinly, and steam until al dente. Add pancetta and zucchini into egg mixture, and mix until blended. Add egg mixture to bacon fat or in olive oil, and cook as instructed.*

Fresh herbs and tomatoes: *Add 2 diced tomatoes and a combination of 3 TBL chopped herbs such as chives, parsley, thyme and basil to egg mixture. Cook as instructed.*

Artichoke and caramelized onions: *Drain and quarter 1 14 oz. can of artichoke hearts, packed in water. In a separate sauté pan, add ½ yellow or any variety of sweet onion, sliced thinly, to 1 TBL olive oil or butter, Sauté for about 3 minutes. Add 1 TBL balsamic vinegar and 1 tsp sugar. Caramelize the liquid, reducing it by ⅓, about 3–5 minutes. Add to egg mixture, and cook as instructed.*

Cannelloni

There is nothing as comforting to an Italian as a Sunday dinner of cannelloni. The soft cylinder of pasta wrapped around finely seasoned meat and cheese and topped with a combination of Marinara and Béchamel sauce is my idea of a beautiful meal. And although this recipe has many parts, it's actually quite easy to prepare. You can use chicken, turkey, beef, Italian sausage or ham as your meat filling. A dairy-free ricotta option makes this dish accessible to everyone.

Ingredients

Prepare one recipe Parmesan Cheese Herb Crepes or dairy-free variation (see page 64)

2 TBL olive oil

1 small onion, chopped

1 clove garlic, minced

1 medium carrot, chopped

1 tsp fresh marjoram, chopped

1 tsp fresh Italian flat-leaf parsley, chopped

½ tsp salt

pinch of pepper

1 lb meat (chicken, turkey, beef, sausage, ham or a combination), skinned and chopped

½ cup red wine

1½ cups Traditional Ricotta Cheese (see page 113)

2 cups Capone's Marinara Sauce (see page 101) or your favorite red sauce

2 cups Capone's Béchamel Sauce (see page 111)

grated Parmesan cheese for garnish

DAIRY-FREE

Substitute *Mary's Dairy-Free Ricotta* (see page 113) for ricotta cheese. Omit Parmesan cheese.

MIX IT UP

PREHEAT OVEN TO 400 DEGREES. LIGHTLY OIL A 9x13" BAKING DISH.

❧ Prepare crepes and set aside.

❧ Heat olive oil over medium heat in a large skillet. Add onion, and cook until translucent, about 3 minutes. Add garlic; cook for about 1 minute. Add carrots, marjoram, parsley, salt and pepper. Cook for an additional 3 minutes.

❧ Add chopped meat. Cook over medium heat until meat browns, about 10 minutes. Add wine, and let it evaporate, about 10 minutes.

❧ Lower heat, cover and cook for an additional 20 minutes or until meat is tender and is cooked through. Salt and pepper to taste.

❧ Add cooked meat mixture to food processor, and pulse until mixture is well-ground.

❧ Add equal amounts of meat topped with ricotta mixture to centers of each of the crepes, and roll into cylinder shapes. Place in the baking dish.

❧ Top with any remaining meat and cheese mixture, and add marinara and/or béchamel sauce. Garnish with Parmesan cheese if desired.

❧ Bake covered for 20 minutes or until flavors are blended and heated through.

Makes 8–10 large cannelloni

Manicotti

Manicotti is the vegetarian equivalent to the meat-filled cannelloni. Similar to cheese ravioli, although lighter in texture, this dish consists of a soft, supple crepe wrapped around a ricotta and spinach filling. I like to cover my manicotti with Capone's Marinara Sauce.

MIX IT UP

PREHEAT OVEN TO 400 DEGREES. LIGHTLY OIL A 9x13" BAKING DISH.

- Prepare crepes and set aside.

- Melt butter in a large skillet over medium high heat. Add spinach, salt and pepper. Stir frequently until spinach is wilted and water has evaporated, about 10 minutes.

- Chop spinach finely with a knife or puree in a blender.

- In a small bowl, mix ricotta, Parmesan, parsley, nutmeg, eggs, salt and pepper until well blended. Stir in spinach.

- Add equal amounts of ricotta-spinach mixture to the center of each of crepe and roll into cylinder shapes. Place in the baking dish. Cover with *Capone's Marinara* or your favorite sauce. Garnish with Parmesan cheese if desired.

- Bake covered for 20 minutes or until filling is heated through. Let rest for 5 minutes before serving.

Makes 8–10 large manicotti

Ingredients

Prepare one recipe Parmesan Cheese Herb Crepes or dairy-free variation (see page 64)

2 TBL butter, ghee or butter alternative

1 cup fresh spinach, washed and trimmed

2 cups ricotta cheese

¼ cup Parmesan cheese

3 TBL fresh Italian flat-leaf parsley, chopped

pinch of nutmeg

2 eggs

salt and pepper to taste

2 cups Capone's Marinara Sauce (see page 101) or your favorite tomato sauce

grated Parmesan cheese for garnish

DAIRY-FREE

Prepare a dairy-free version of crepes, and substitute a double batch of *Mary's Dairy Free Ricotta* (see page 113) for ricotta cheese. Omit Parmesan cheese.

Melanzane alla Parmigiana

EGGPLANT PARMESAN

A simple dish of lightly battered eggplant and sauce with a little cheese goes a long way in setting a truly authentic Italian table. Although this dish could be considered an appetizer, I like to add a mixed green salad and a loaf of gluten-free focaccia bread to make it a complete dinner.

Ingredients

1 large purple globed eggplant, thinly sliced

3 TBL tapioca flour, plus more if needed

1 cup gluten-free bread crumbs

2–3 eggs, beaten

olive oil for frying or drizzling

3 cups Capone's Marinara Sauce (see page 101) or your favorite tomato sauce

½ cup Parmesan cheese, grated

8 oz. fresh mozzarella cheese, sliced

3 TBL fresh basil, chopped

salt and pepper to taste

DAIRY-FREE

Use dairy-free mozzarella cheese, omit Parmesan cheese and salt to taste.

MIX IT UP

PREHEAT OVEN TO 375 DEGREES. SET OUT A 9x9" BAKING DISH.

❧ Slice eggplant into ¼" thick slices. Place slices in a single layer on paper towels. Sprinkle with salt. Let stand for 30 minutes. Blot moisture and excess salt from the eggplant.

❧ On 2 separate plates, add tapioca flour and bread crumbs.

❧ Lightly beat 2–3 eggs in a medium bowl.

❧ For frying: Heat olive oil in a large skillet. Dust eggplant with tapioca flour, dip in egg, and pat onto plate of gluten-free bread crumbs. Add to hot oil, and fry until golden brown, about 3–5 minutes, turning once. Place on a paper towel-lined plate. Salt to taste.

❧ For baking: line 2 baking sheets with parchment paper. Dress the eggplant as above, and place in a single layer on the baking sheet. Drizzle olive oil over the top, and sprinkle with sea salt. Bake in a 375-degree oven until tender, about 15 minutes.

❧ Ladle ¼ cup of the sauce into the baking dish. Add eggplant pieces in a single layer. Add another ladle of sauce to the top, and sprinkle with about 2 TBL Parmesan cheese, about ¼ of the mozzarella and 1 TBL basil. Repeat the process until all the ingredients are used up. Cover the top with the remaining sauce, sprinkle with remaining cheese and decorate with a full basil leaf.

❧ Bake in oven covered with a tightly fitting lid or foil for about 20–25 minutes, or until cheese is melted and sauce is bubbling. Let set for 5 minutes.

Serves 4

Lasagne con Funghi e Verdura
WILD MUSHROOM AND VEGETABLE LASAGNA

Every autumn, my Uncle Joe would venture into the woods and wildcraft beautiful mushrooms, which my Aunt Carmel would turn into a peppery dish. You can serve this mushroom lasagna with Capone's Marinara Sauce or Capone's Béchamel Sauce. I like to use a combination of both.

MIX IT UP

PREHEAT OVEN TO 375 DEGREES. SET OUT A 9x13" BAKING DISH.

❧ Prepare Parmesan Cheese Herb Crepes and set aside.

❧ Slice mozzarella into ¼" slices.

❧ In a medium bowl, combine ricotta cheese, cream, basil, ¼ cup parmesan cheese, salt, pepper, and nutmeg. Mix until creamy.

❧ Heat olive oil in a large skillet over medium heat. Add garlic; sauté for 1 minute. Add pepper slices, and sauté about 3 minutes.

❧ Add mushrooms, zucchini, marjoram, sea salt and pepper. Sauté until mushrooms are golden brown and veggies are *al dente*. Add wine; reduce until all the liquid is absorbed, about 5 minutes. Set aside.

❧ Add ½ cup sauce such as *Capone's Marinara* or *Béchamel* or a combination of each to the baking dish.

❧ Lay 2 crepes end to end, covering the bottom of the dish. Spread ½ cup of sauce, ⅓ of the mushroom filling, ⅓ of the mozzarella and ricotta cheese filling, and then sprinkle with some of the remaining Parmesan cheese. Add 2 more crepes and repeat the process. Top off with the last 2 crepes, add any remaining mozzarella and ricotta cheese, and sprinkle with Parmesan cheese.

❧ Cover with foil, and bake 30–40 minutes or until lasagna is thoroughly heated. Remove from oven, and let rest uncovered for 15 minutes. Cut into squares and serve.

Serves 6–8

Ingredients

Add to Parmesan Cheese Herb Crepes or dairy-free variation (see page 64)

8 oz. fresh mozzarella

1 cup ricotta cheese

3 TBL cream, light cream or milk

2 TBL fresh basil, chopped

1 cup Parmesan cheese, finely grated

salt and pepper to taste

pinch of nutmeg

2 TBL olive oil

2 cloves garlic, minced

1 red, orange or yellow pepper, sliced

¼ lb. shitake mushrooms

¼ lb. porcini mushrooms

1 lb. crimini mushrooms

1 medium zucchini, thinly sliced

½ tsp fresh marjoram

½ tsp sea salt and pepper to taste

1 cup dry red or white wine

DAIRY-FREE

Substitute *Mary's Dairy-Free Ricotta* (see page 113), and add ¼ cup toasted pine nuts. Substitute milk alternative for cream. Top with mozzarella alternative.

MAMA CAPONE'S TRADITIONAL LASAGNA

My mother is the lasagna-maker in our family. Her recipe calls for pasta ribbons layered with a mixture of rich cheeses and buried in a meaty tomato sauce. Cut into perfect squares, you could see one layer of delicious filling melting into the next. Although this recipe requires several dishes to be made ahead, once that is done, putting together the main event is quite easy. And with the gluten-free crepe pasta, Mama Capone's Lasagna is back on the menu.

Ingredients

Capone's Marinara Sauce (see page 101) or your favorite meat sauce

8 Parmesan Herb Crepes (see page 64) or dairy-free crepes

½ lb. Italian sausage such as pork, turkey or chicken, casing removed and cut into 1" pieces

½ lb. ground beef

15 oz. ricotta cheese

1 large egg

2 TBL fresh Italian flat-leaf parsley, finely chopped

3 TBL cream, light cream or milk

1 cup Parmesan cheese, finely grated

salt and pepper to taste

pinch of nutmeg

1 lb. mozzarella cheese, sliced ¼" thick

3 TBL fresh basil, finely chopped

DAIRY-FREE

Make dairy-free crepes and *Mary's Dairy-Free Ricotta* (see page 113). Substitute milk alternative for cream. Top with mozzarella alternative.

MIX IT UP

PREHEAT OVEN TO 350 DEGREES. SET OUT A 9x13" BAKING DISH.

❧ Prepare *Capone's Marinara* and crepes. These can be made a day ahead and refrigerated.

❧ In a large sauté pan over medium heat, add sausage and beef. Brown all sides, about 5–7 minutes. Transfer to a paper towel-lined dish and let cool.

❧ In a medium bowl, combine ricotta cheese, egg, parsley, cream, ¼ cup Parmesan cheese, salt, pepper and nutmeg. Mix until creamy.

❧ Lay out all your prepared ingredients in front of you in this order: Capone's Marinara, crepes, meat, ricotta, mozzarella cheese, Parmesan cheese and chopped basil.

❧ Add a ladle of sauce to coat the bottom of the baking dish. Add 2 crepes end-to-end, covering the bottom of the pan. Spread ¼ of the meat mixture over the crepe layer.

❧ Next, add a heaping tablespoon of ricotta and spread lightly over the meat, about 3–4 TBL per layer. Add mozzarella slices, spacing them evenly, about 2" apart. Sprinkle 3 TBL of Parmesan cheese over the top. Then scatter 1 TBL of fresh basil over the layer.

❧ Repeat process for 3 more layers, ending with crepes on top. On this layer add sauce and a little Parmesan cheese, as well as any left-over ricotta or mozzarella. Finish with a sprinkle of chopped basil.

❧ Bake covered with foil 30–40 minutes or until ingredients are bubbling. Remove from oven, and let rest 15 minutes before cutting.

Serves 8–10

PANCETTA, ARUGULA AND TOMATO SANDWICH

Sometimes the simplest dinners offer the greatest satisfaction. On baking days, I love to make this Italian style panini sandwich. When I was growing up, the bacon in our house was pancetta. Thinly sliced and baked in the oven, it makes this BLT deliciously different. Try the red curry mayonnaise to send it over the top.

MIX IT UP

PREHEAT OVEN TO 400 DEGREES. LINE A BAKING SHEET WITH PARCHMENT PAPER.

🍃 Cut pancetta slices in half and lay them on the prepared baking sheet. Bake 10 minutes or until pancetta is crispy.

🍃 In a small bowl, mix together mayonnaise, curry paste, capers and onion. Set aside.

🍃 Slice bread or cut rolls lengthwise. Toast lightly if desired. Add 1 tablespoon of curry mayonnaise to each of the bread slices.

🍃 Evenly divide pancetta, tomato slices and arugula between bread slices.

Serves 4

Ingredients

8 slices pancetta, thinly sliced

½ cup mayonnaise

2 tsp Thai Kitchen red curry paste (more if desired)

2 TBL capers

¼ cup red onion, diced small

2 ripe tomatoes, sliced

2 cups arugula or mixed baby greens

8 slices gluten-free bread or 4 gluten-free Panino rolls, lightly toasted (see page 58)

BRAISED PORK LOIN WITH APRICOT GRAVY

On one of my visits to Italy, I hiked with a friend in the beautiful Italian Alps. After nearly two hours of ascension, we reached a refugeo, a sort of lodge that sat on the edge of a beautiful alpine lake, surrounded by pine trees and rising peaks. Others hikers, like us, were enjoying the lake; some were fishing, some simply admiring the beauty. Around dusk, to my surprise, a stout, bearded man came out of the refugeo and rang a triangle bell, calling everyone in for dinner. We folded into the beautiful wood cabin interior and were greeted by a roaring fire and this meal.

Ingredients

1 cup apricots, halved

1 cup wine such as port or a sweet white wine

3 cloves garlic, chopped

2 sprigs fresh rosemary, stemmed

1 tsp lavender flowers (optional)

2–3 lb. pork loin roast, bone-in French cut

3 TBL tapioca flour

3 TBL olive oil

2 carrots, chopped

1 onion, chopped

2 stalks celery, chopped

½ lb. wild mushrooms such as shitake, oyster, morels or crimini, sliced

3 cups broth such as mushroom, beef or onion broth

1 cup heavy cream

salt and pepper to taste

Add to one basic or herb polenta recipe (see page 160 or 140)

MIX IT UP

🍃 Add apricot halves to wine. Soak for 1 hour.

🍃 In a small bowl, or with a mortar and pestle, combine garlic, rosemary and lavender flowers.

🍃 To prepare the meat, have your butcher French-cut a bone-in pork loin, or remove the fat around the bones. Not only is your roast prettier, it helps with the cutting of individual chops when plating the meal.

🍃 Pat meat dry with a paper towel. Turn the roast with bones facing down, and with a paring knife make 1" slits in the meat throughout the roast. Stuff each slit with a little of the rosemary, garlic and lavender flowers mix.

🍃 Salt and pepper the outside generously. Lightly dust all sides of meat with tapioca flour

🍃 In a large saucepan or stock pot, heat olive oil over medium high heat. Add meat, sear or brown on each side for 4 minutes or until meat pulls away easily from the pan. Make sure to brown the edges and ends of the pork loin. When meat is browned on all sides, remove from pan and set aside.

🍃 Add carrots, onion, and celery to stock pot, and sauté until *al dente*, about 3 minutes. Add mushrooms and the wine used to marinate the apricots (saving apricots for later) to the pot and reduce, about 5 minutes.

continued

MIX IT UP *continued*

Return pork loin to the pot with large side down, and add broth until it reaches about halfway up the meat.

Cover and simmer meat in the broth for 1¼– 1½ hours, rotating the meat every 25 minutes or so. Cook all sides in broth, including the ends. Using a meat thermometer (130 degrees = rare, 140 degrees = medium, 150 degrees = well-done), remove meat to a cutting board when desired internal temperature is reached.

With a slotted spoon, transfer vegetables to a serving bowl and keep warm.

Reduce broth by half and then add heavy cream and the marinated apricots.

Cut pork loin in between bones to create individual chops. Start by plating prepared polenta first, then a ladle of vegetables, next the chop, and finally a ladle of the apricot cream sauce. Serve immediately with extra sauce for the table.

Serves 6

SAUSAGE AND HERB POLENTA

This meal is hearty and especially comforting on a cool autumn or winter night. I like to serve this dish with the sausages nestled in a bed of polenta, and add herb popovers and a seasonal vegetable dish.

Ingredients: Herb polenta

4 cups cold water, divided

1 cup yellow or white cornmeal (preferably stone ground)

2 tsp salt

2 TBL fresh oregano, or 1 TBL fresh sage, chopped

3 TBL fresh Italian flat-leaf parsley, chopped

2 TBL butter, ghee or butter alternative

Ingredients: Sausage

1½ lbs. sausage such as Italian pork, chicken or turkey sausage, or a combination

2 TBL olive oil

1 TBL butter, ghee or butter alternative

2 TBL balsamic vinegar

MIX IT UP: HERB POLENTA

✎ In a medium saucepan, bring 3 cups of the cold water to a boil.

✎ In a small bowl, mix cornmeal, salt, oregano, parsley and remaining 1 cup cold water.

✎ Add cornmeal mix to boiling water, and lower heat to low or until the mixture stays at a moderate boil. Stir with a wooden spoon almost constantly for 30–40 minutes. Polenta will thicken and begin to leave the sides of the pan.

✎ Stir in butter, and plate on a round dish making a "bird's nest" in the center for the sausages.

MIX IT UP: SAUSAGE

✎ Gently remove casings from the sausages, and cut into 4" pieces. Removing the casings makes the sausages tender.

✎ Heat the olive oil and butter in a large skillet over medium heat. Add sausages and cook slowly for 10–15 minutes until sausages are done and firm to the touch.

✎ Remove sausages to plated polenta, adding them to the center of the bird's nest. Keep warm in the oven. Add balsamic vinegar to the pan with the drippings and reduce by half, about 3 minutes.

✎ Pour reduced balsamic sauce over sausage and polenta. Serve immediately.

Serves 6

Salsiccia e Capsicums
SAUSAGE AND PEPPERS

When I was growing up, a plentiful platter of sausage and peppers made it to every large family gathering. And why not? Italian sausage mixed with sweet bell peppers and onions in a tomato basil sauce is a remarkable dish. Serve this savory selection on a gluten-free panino roll, gluten-free bread or focaccia. It's also great all by itself on a plate — just make sure you eat it with a spoon to get every last drop!

MIX IT UP

≈ In a large skillet, heat olive oil over medium heat. Add onion. Sauté until translucent, about 3 minutes. Add peppers and garlic, and sauté until peppers begin to soften, about 5–7 minutes.

≈ Add sausage, parsley and basil; cook uncovered until sausage begins to brown, about 10 minutes.

≈ Lower heat and add tomatoes, sea salt and pepper, and simmer for 20 minutes or until sausage is cooked through.

≈ Serve with gluten-free bread and Parmesan cheese for garnish, if desired.

Serves 6

Ingredients

2 TBL olive oil

1 large onion, thinly sliced

4 red, orange or yellow bell peppers, cored and thinly sliced

3 cloves garlic, chopped

1 lb. hot or mild Italian sausage, casing removed and cut into bite-size pieces

1 TBL fresh Italian flat-leaf parsley, chopped

1 TBL fresh basil, chopped

1 14 oz. can whole tomatoes, chopped and liquid reserved

¼ tsp or more sea salt

fresh ground pepper to taste

Parmesan cheese for garnish (optional)

Bistecca alla Pizzaiola

PIZZA STEAK

My father put sauce and grated cheese on everything. Meats, vegetables and stews were often topped with a tempting dab of tomato sauce, a drizzle of olive oil and a pile of freshly grated cheese, turning everything into a variegated pizza. Here's one of my favorite ways to enjoy steak: pizza-style. Have your butcher cut your steaks for you to make this a super-easy meal.

Ingredients

2 TBL olive oil

6 pieces steak such as flank or skirt steak, beef round or top sirloin, thinly sliced

2 cloves garlic, peeled and smashed

1 14 oz. can whole tomatoes, chopped

¼ cup dry red wine (optional)

2 TBL fresh oregano, finely chopped

grated Pecorino Romano cheese for garnish

MIX IT UP

In a large skillet, heat olive oil over medium high heat. Add steaks and cook on one side until brown, about 4 minutes or less depending on the thickness. Then turn and cook on the other side about 3 minutes.

Add garlic; cook for 2 minutes. Lower heat, and add tomatoes, wine (if desired) and oregano. Simmer until the sauce reduces and thickens, about 20 minutes.

Transfer steak to a platter, cover with sauce and sprinkle with Pecorino Romano cheese.

Serves 6

POPPIE'S MEATBALLS

This is my father's meatball recipe. He insisted the secret to a great meatball was to mix everything with your hands. We seemed to always have a great supply of these tasty morsels in our refrigerator, and they served as a way of introduction in our household. The first thing my father would ask any friends I brought home was; "Hey, you want a meatball sandwich?" Hardly anyone refused.

MIX IT UP

PREHEAT OVEN TO 350 DEGREES. LIGHTLY GREASE A BAKING SHEET.

❧ In a large mixing bowl, add all ingredients and mix with your hands for the best results. Smell the mixture to see if it smells flavorful enough. Add more salt and pepper, grated cheese or herbs if the mixture smells too bland.

❧ Form into 2–3" meatballs, rolling them lightly in you hands just until they form balls.

❧ Place meatballs on the baking sheet and bake 20 minutes.

❧ Add to *Capone's Marinara Sauce* or your favorite tomato sauce. Serve with your choice of gluten-free pasta, gnudi, gnocchi or polenta. Or add to a panino roll and enjoy a meatball sandwich.

Makes 12

Ingredients

1 lb. ground beef (85% fat)

1 egg

¾ cup homemade gluten-free bread crumbs

¼ cup pine nuts

2 cloves garlic, minced

½ cup yellow onion, minced

¼ cup fresh Italian flat-leaf parsley, chopped (or 2 TBL dried)

¼ cup fresh basil, chopped (or 2 TBL dried)

½ cup Parmesan cheese, finely grated

½ tsp or more salt

pepper to taste

DAIRY-FREE

Substitute toasted and minced walnuts or pine nuts for Parmesan cheese, and increase salt to 1 teaspoon.

Braciole

STUFFED FLANK STEAK

My great grandmother came for Sorrento, a charming hillside city in southern Italy that tumbles to the sea. This is her family's version of braciole, a tender steak roll stuffed with toasted pine nuts, herbs and spices. I can't help thinking that her addition of sweet raisins was inspired by the sweetness of her view. I like to add a fresh, simple sauce of tomatoes and herbs to the top, but feel free to add a cup of Capone's Marinara if it's already prepared. I use flank steak, sometimes called skirt steak, for the most tender results. Have your butcher slice it thin.

Ingredients

1 lb. steak such as flank or skirt steak (bottom round or top round can be used), pounded to ½" thick, cut into 6 pieces

3 cloves garlic, minced

3 TBL fresh Italian flat-leaf parsley, finely chopped

3 TBL basil, finely chopped

2 TBL raisins

¼ cut pine nuts, toasted

½ cup Parmesan cheese, grated (optional)

salt and pepper

kitchen string for tying

olive oil for frying

1 TBL olive oil

2 cloves garlic, chopped

2 TBL fresh basil, chopped

4 plum tomatoes, chopped

salt and pepper to taste

MIX IT UP

PREHEAT OVEN TO 350 DEGREES. LIGHTLY GREASE A 9x13" BAKING DISH.

❧ Cut steak into 6 pieces, and pound it out with a meat tenderizer until meat is about ½" thick. Set aside.

❧ In a small bowl, combine garlic, parsley, basil, raisins, pine nuts and Parmesan cheese.

❧ Pat meat dry with paper towel, and salt and pepper both sides. Spoon equal amounts of filling in the center of the steak pieces. Roll steak into a cylinder shape and tie each piece with kitchen string.

❧ Heat a skillet large enough to fit all of the meat without crowding on medium high heat for about 3 minutes. Add olive oil and warm for another minute. Add steak rolls to hot oil, and sear meat until bottom is well browned and can turn easily. If the meat sticks, it is not ready to be moved. Finish searing, then rotate to the next side. When steak is finished browning, place in the baking dish.

❧ For fresh sauce, heat oil in a medium saucepan over medium heat, and add garlic and basil. Sauté 1 minute. Add tomatoes, salt and pepper, and cook 8–10 minutes until tomatoes form a light sauce.

❧ Add sauce to the top of the *braciole*, and sprinkle with Parmesan cheese if desired. Cover and bake about 10 minutes.

Serves 6

TUFFY LEVO'S BRAISED BEEF RIBS

Although my grandfather took this recipe with him to his grave (his nickname wasn't Tuffy for nothing), the family put their collective memory together and came up with this rendition of his famous, tantalizing ribs. I like to serve these over whipped white or sweet potatoes, or creamy polenta. You'll want something to catch the sauce.

MIX IT UP

Heat olive oil in a large saucepan or stock pot over medium high heat. Salt and pepper the short ribs, and dust them with tapioca flour on all sides. Add to pan and brown on all sides, about 3–4 minutes per side. Turn down the heat if necessary.

Remove beef ribs and place on platter. Reduce heat to medium. Add onions to remaining oil and meat drippings; cook until opaque, about 3 minutes. Add carrots and celery, and sauté for about 3 minutes. Add garlic, rosemary, thyme, salt, pepper and wine. Let the wine reduce in half, about 5 minutes.

Add tomatoes, reserved tomato juice, beef broth, wine and peas; return to simmer. Add beef ribs to sauce and cover. Simmer slowly for 1½ hours or until the meat falls from the bone. Adjust spices and salt and pepper as you go.

Transfer ribs to a platter, and skim the top of sauce to remove any excess fat. Uncover pot, and reduce sauce by half, simmering about 20 minutes.

Serve with a layer of potatoes or polenta, beef ribs and then a ladle of ragu over the top.

Serves 4

Ingredients

2 TBL olive oil
3–4 lbs. beef short ribs
¼ cup tapioca flour
2 medium yellow onions, diced
2 carrots, diced
2 stalks celery, diced
5 cloves garlic, smashed
3–4 sprigs fresh rosemary, stemmed and finely chopped
4 sprigs fresh thyme, stemmed and finely chopped
1 cup dry red wine
1 28 oz. can whole tomatoes, chopped, tomato juice reserved
2 cups beef broth
1 cup frozen peas
sea salt and pepper to taste

THE GLUTEN-FREE ITALIAN COOKBOOK

145

Le Verdure

VEGETABLES AND SIDE DISHES

Le Verdure

*M*y father's family comes from the South of Italy near Naples, in a small town called Pontelatone. The town still functions much in the same way it has for over 50 years. Walled off to automobiles with a brightly painted church in its center *piazza*, it displays a pale blue fountain that has not worked since it was bombed in World War II. Here, the villagers live a quiet, agrarian life. Most of the young people have moved north to Milano in the quest for jobs and a modern lifestyle.

The older generation still work in their fields and wait for the street vendors to arrive on their motor scooters, pulling small trailers behind them, and singing their offerings into a microphone. On Tuesday the fruit vendor passes through. On Thursdays it is the song of the vendor who sells *oliva* (olives) and *formaggio* (cheese) that fills the air. Once a month, the sheepherder guides his gentle, bleating flock through the narrow winding streets.

They live simply, producing most of their foods in their courtyard gardens, eating well on the fresh foods of the season. When I visit, I am reminded of the provincial meals of Southern Italians: beans and pasta with a light tomato sauce, rice and peas, sautéed greens with an amaretto cookie crumble, simple fresh salads. For the most of the year, my relatives live on lovely vegetable dishes with legumes, pastas and grains thrown in. But on special occasions, like when I arrived for the first time, they slaughter a pig, using each and every part of it in some fine culinary dish.

This section is devoted to *le verdure*, the unassuming vegetable dish that can easily be cast as a main course. Unlike my Italian relatives, I have a small garden of mostly herbs, with a few pepper and tomato plants. I hardly produce enough to feed a family of four. Instead, I shop at the farmer's markets and local stands, enjoying the freshest food of the seasons. I might choose to blanch or a lightly sauté my prized purchases, or even bake them slowly, packing them with a delectable stuffing. And all summer long, I am called to fresh greens, which I enjoy in a variety of salads. When autumn comes around, I buy crates of tomatoes, onions, peppers, eggplant and squash from the farmer's market. I combine them with my remaining garden herbs and blanch or stew them, packing my freezer full.

In the section, we honor *le verdure*, the vegetable, for its ability to add color to our tables — and to our palates, exquisite taste.

Insalata Mediterranean

MIXED GREEN MEDITERRANEAN SALAD

Insalata Mediterranean is my version of a compound mixed green salad. I like to start with a head of Boston lettuce, and Romaine lettuce, arugula and some fresh herbs such as whole basil leaves. This recipe is good for any time of year since many of the items are readily available as prepared condiments. I like to finish my insalata with Mary's Vinaigrette.

MIX IT UP

➤ Clean all greens and herbs, and either run the greens through a salad spinner or let them drain thoroughly in a colander. It is important for the salad to be dry in order for the dressing to coat the leaves.

➤ Place greens in a large bowl, and toss with *Mary's Vinaigrette* (see page 153) or your own salad dressing. Decorate top with tomatoes, red peppers, sun dried tomatoes and olives, and garnish with cheese. Serve immediately.

Makes 6

Ingredients

1 head Boston butter lettuce

½ head romaine lettuce

¼ cup arugula

¼ cup whole fresh basil leaves

1 cup grape or cherry tomatoes

½ cup roasted red peppers, thinly sliced

⅛ cup sun dried tomatoes, sliced

¼ cup Calamata olives

shaved Parmesan cheese for garnish

Insalata Prosciutto e Rucola

ARUGULA-PROSCIUTTO ORANGE WALNUT SALAD

Arugula is making a strong comeback. This slightly bitter, peppery green makes a tangy and refreshing salad when combined with the salty snap of prosciutto and the sweetness of blood oranges. I like to top this salad with a citrus vinaigrette. If blood oranges are hard to find, use Valencia or your favorite variety.

Ingredients

1 tsp butter, ghee or butter alternative

½ cup walnuts, chopped

1 TBL golden brown sugar

2 large blood oranges, peeled and separated

12 thin slices prosciutto

¼ lb. arugula leaves, washed and dried

2 TBL fresh-squeezed blood orange juice

orange zest

1 tsp balsamic vinegar

1 TBL fresh Italian flat-leaf parsley, stemmed and chopped

¼ cup olive oil

salt and pepper to taste

MIX IT UP

In a medium skillet, melt butter over medium heat. Add walnuts; toast for about 1 minute. Add sugar, and toast walnuts until light brown and aromatic, about 2 minutes. Transfer to a plate or baking sheet to cool.

Set out 6 cold salad plates. Divide the orange slices among the plates, and top each plate with 2 slices of prosciutto.

In a blender, add orange juice, zest, vinegar, salt, pepper and herbs. Pulse until blended. In a slow, steady stream, add olive oil until the mixture emulsifies or becomes thick and thoroughly blended.

Toss arugula with enough vinaigrette to lightly coat, and add to the top of the salad plates. Top with candied walnuts. Serve cold.

Serves 6

Insalata all'Acciugata
ENDIVE WITH ANCHOVIES AND HAZELNUTS

My Aunt Carmel always had a large bowl of endive salad at her table mixed with a light vinaigrette. Just for fun, I have added white anchovies and toasted hazelnuts to these flavorful greens.

MIX IT UP

Trim and wash endive, and dry thoroughly. Place in a salad bowl.

In a medium skillet, toast hazelnuts until light brown and aromatic, about 3 minutes. Remove from heat. Add to salad when cooled slightly.

Add anchovies and Grana Padana cheese to the top of the salad.

In a small bowl, mix balsamic vinegar and sea salt. Stir until sea salt dissolves and add olive oil. Shake or whisk to combine. Sprinkle over salad, and mix well to coat evenly.

Divide evenly among 6 salad plates, and top with additional Grana Padano cheese shavings.

Serves 6

Ingredients

1 head Belgian endive

¼ cup hazelnuts, chopped

6 white anchovy fillets, packed in oil, chopped

2 oz. Grana Padano cheese, shaved with cheese knife or grater, plus more for garnish

1 TBL balsamic vinegar

¼ tsp sea salt

¼ cup olive oil

 LE VERDURE

Asparagi Con Burro e Limone

ASPARAGUS WITH LEMON THYME BUTTER

Although asparagus used to be strictly a spring affair, it is now offered in markets almost year-round. The addition of thyme, lemon and butter to this dish makes it refreshing and delicious.

Ingredients

1 lb. asparagus, trimmed

3 TBL butter, ghee or butter alternative

1 tsp fresh thyme, stemmed and chopped

1 TBL fresh lemon juice

¼ cup Parmesan cheese, grated

fresh ground pepper to taste

DAIRY-FREE

Substitute toasted sesame seeds for Parmesan cheese, and add a pinch of sea salt.

MIX IT UP

✎ Blanch asparagus in a pot of rapidly boiling salted water until crisp and tender, about 3 minutes. Transfer to a platter.

✎ Heat butter over medium heat in a small saucepan. Add thyme and lemon juice, and simmer until butter is a light brown.

✎ Pour over asparagus, and sprinkle with Parmesan cheese and pepper. Serve warm.

Serves 4

MARY'S VINAIGRETTE

I always have a jar of this dressing in the refrigerator. My family demands it. This vinaigrette is great for salads or as a marinade for a variety of dishes.

MIX IT UP

〰 Combine all ingredients in a salad dressing container with a lid. Shake until incorporated. Taste and season to your liking. Add more Braggs if you like it a little saltier. Add more lemon or vinegar for increased tartness. Or add more olive oil to neutralize the overall taste.

〰 For a simple salad, rinse and dry mixed greens. Add just enough dressing to coat. Toss and serve.

Makes 1 cup

Ingredients

½ cup olive oil

¼ cup Bragg's Liquid Aminos

½ lemon, squeezed

2 TBL balsamic vinegar

1 cloves garlic, minced

fresh ground pepper

Chef's Notes

Bragg's Liquid Aminos is a vegetable protein from non-fermented soybeans. I like to use it in as a gluten-free alternative to fermented soy sauce.

BRAISED RADICCHIO WITH PANCETTA BALSAMIC VINEGAR REDUCTION

Radicchio, or Belgian endive, is a vegetable that is beloved by Italians. Grown in Italian gardens since the 1800s, it literally translates as "chicory." It is a slightly bitter vegetable, perfect in winter when the green leaves turn a rich red. It takes only minutes to prepare and adds both color and a traditional Italian flavor to your meal. And don't let the bitter taste put you off. The longer you cook it, the sweeter it becomes.

Ingredients

1 TBL olive oil

3 slices pancetta

3 TBL balsamic vinegar

1 TBL sugar

1 lb. radicchio (or 1 head), cut in wedges with outer leaves and core removed

salt and pepper to taste

MIX IT UP

❧ Over medium low heat, warm olive oil in a large skillet. Add pancetta slices. Sauté until pancetta takes on color, about 5 minutes.

❧ Add balsamic vinegar and sugar, and reduce until sauce thickens, about 7–10 minutes.

❧ Add radicchio wedges; braise in sauce, turning gently for 5–7 minutes or until leaves are wilted.

❧ Transfer wedges to a serving platter, and pour sauce over the top.

Serves 6

Bietoline Alle Petti

SAUTÉED BEET GREENS WITH WALNUTS

Fresh greens of the season always find their way into our kitchen in the form of light sautéed dishes, or in a steaming pot of soup. In this recipe you can use beet greens, Swiss chard, mustard greens or spinach.

MIX IT UP

In a large skillet, heat olive oil and butter over medium heat. Add garlic and walnuts; cook until light brown, about 1 minute.

Add beet greens, salt and pepper. Lightly sauté just until wilted and coated in oil, about 3 minutes. Transfer to a platter, and serve warm.

Serves 6

Ingredients

1 TBL olive oil

1 TBL butter, ghee or butter alternative

1 clove garlic, chopped

¼ cup walnuts, chopped

1 ½ lbs. fresh beet greens, Swiss chard, mustard greens or spinach

salt and pepper to taste

Spinaci con Amaretti

SAUTÉED SPINACH WITH ALMOND COOKIES

This spinach dish requires that you share a few of your Amaretti, or almond cookies (see page 174). When I make Amaretti, I freeze 3–4 for this particular reason. The salty-and-sweet combination of this dish makes the cookie sacrifice well worth it. In a pinch, you can substitute store-bought gluten-free biscotti.

Ingredients

1 lb. spinach, washed and dried

2 TBL butter or olive oil

3–4 almond cookies

salt and pepper to taste

MIX IT UP

☞ Melt butter in a large skillet over medium-high heat. Add spinach, salt and pepper to taste, and sauté until spinach is wilted and slightly dry, about 3–5 minutes.

☞ Transfer to a platter, and crumble almond cookies over the top. Serve immediately.

Serves 6

Broccoli Freddo

COLD BROCCOLI SALAD

Broccoli freddo is a cold broccoli preparation that makes a tasty dish for summer picnics or as an ingredient on a cold antipasto platter. And it's a great way to use steamed broccoli leftovers.

MIX IT UP

Wash the broccoli, and remove all but 3" of the stem. Peel the remaining tough outer stem, and cut broccoli into spears lengthwise.

Steam until easily pierced with a fork. Transfer to a bowl and drizzle with olive oil, salt, garlic and lemon. Mix until coated and refrigerate, covered, for several hours. Can be made a day ahead of time. Serve cold.

Serves 6

Ingredients

1 lb. broccoli, stems peeled and cut into spears

¼ cup olive oil

pinch of salt

1 clove garlic, minced

½ lemon, juiced

Cime di Rapa
BROCCOLI RAPINI

In my family, broccoli rapini, or broccoli raab, was served lightly sautéed with pine nuts and raisins. You can add a little lemon and/or a pinch of red pepper flakes for extra flavor.

Ingredients

1–2 TBL olive oil

½ lb. broccoli rapini

2 cloves garlic, chopped

¼ cup pine nuts

2 TBL raisins

pinch of red pepper flakes (optional)

1 tsp lemon juice (optional)

salt and pepper to taste

MIX IT UP

In a sauté pan, heat olive oil over medium high heat. Add broccoli rapini and garlic to hot oil, and sauté for 2 minutes. Add pine nuts and raisins. Sauté for an additional 2 minutes.

Add salt and pepper, and red pepper and lemon if desired.

Remove from heat. Serve warm or at room temperature.

Serves 4

Chef's Notes

Make sure you buy broccoli rapini, also called raab, rapine or rabe. Broccoli rapini is actually not a member of the broccoli family but is more akin to turnip greens with lots of broccoli-like buds.

Fagiolini Alla Mandorle
GREEN BEANS WITH ALMONDS

This recipe is one of my family's favorites. Although I use a little gluten-free soy sauce in this dish, I still consider it an excellent Italian side dish.

MIX IT UP

In a large skillet, heat olive oil and butter over medium heat. Add green beans, almonds, pepper and gluten-free soy sauce. Sauté, turning every few minutes until green beans are *al dente*, or crisp but tender, about 12–15 minutes.

Transfer to a platter, and serve warm.

Serves 4–6

Ingredients

1 TBL olive oil

1 TBL butter, ghee or butter alternative

1 lb. green beans, ends trimmed

¼ cup almonds, chopped

2 TBL gluten-free soy sauce such as Bragg Liquid Aminos

pepper to taste

Soy-free variation

Substitute 1 TBL balsamic vinegar for the gluten-free soy sauce.

BASIC POLENTA

Polenta was first introduced to Italy from the New World in the 16th century. The Italians welcomed it into their diets, creating many delectable dishes. From the north came a full-flavored yellow polenta, which was served with braised meats and sauces. Veneto brought us the creamy white polenta, excellent with fish and poultry. Like risotto, polenta requires constant stirring and monitoring for 30 minutes or so.

Ingredients

4 cups cold water, divided

1 cup polenta or coarse yellow or fine white cornmeal (preferably stone ground)

2 tsp salt

2 TBL butter, ghee or butter alternative

Chef's Notes

I sometimes order online a finely ground cornmeal called *Sala Cereali*. *Sala Cereali* is precooked and finely ground very much like an instant oatmeal and cooks in 5 minutes. It makes this delicious polenta side dish much easier.

MIX IT UP

➥ In a medium saucepan, bring 3 cups of the water to a boil.

➥ In a small bowl, mix cornmeal, salt and the remaining 1 cup water.

➥ Add cornmeal mix to boiling water, and lower heat until the mixture stays at a moderate boil. Stir with a wooden spoon almost constantly for 30–40 minutes. When done, polenta will thicken and begin to leave the sides of the pan.

➥ Stir in butter, and serve immediately.

Serves 6

Patate Con Rosmarino

NEW POTATOES WITH ROSEMARY

My sister Angela shared her secret to her roasted potatoes. Just remember to peel a strip around the potato to allow the seasonings to layer in while still enjoying the crispy skin. You can substitute parsley, oregano and/or marjoram for the rosemary.

MIX IT UP

PREHEAT OVEN TO 450 DEGREES. SET OUT A 9″ SQUARE BAKING DISH.

⌇ Wash potatoes, and peel one strip of skin around the center of the potato, about 1½″ wide.

⌇ Place potatoes in the baking dish and add olive oil, rosemary, sea salt, pepper and capers (if desired). Toss to coat.

⌇ Turn potatoes once during the baking cycle, coating again with the oil mixture. Remove from the oven when potatoes are easily pieced with fork and golden brown, about 35–40 minutes.

⌇ Transfer to a platter, and serve immediately.

Serves 4–6

Ingredients

12 new potatoes

3 TBL olive oil (or 2 TBL oil and 1 TBL butter or butter alternative)

2 sprigs fresh rosemary, stemmed and finely chopped

¼ tsp sea salt

3 TBL capers, well-drained (optional)

pepper to taste

Patate alle Cipolle e Funghi

SCALLOPED POTATOES WITH MUSHROOMS AND ONIONS

I like to serve this simple dairy-free side dish with fish or meat. Sometimes I serve it as the main course with a mixed green salad.

Ingredients

2 TBL olive oil (or butter and olive oil mixture)

½ lb. wild mushrooms such as shitake, crimini, oyster, cleaned and sliced

1 tsp salt

3 TBL fresh herbs such as thyme, Italian flat-leaf parsley, sage or a combination, stemmed and chopped

3 white, red or yellow potatoes, peeled and sliced in ¼" wedges

1 large yellow onion, thinly sliced

2 sweet potatoes, peeled and sliced in ¼" wedges

4 TBL butter, ghee or butter alternative

1 cup milk or unsweetened milk alternative

pinch of nutmeg

fresh ground pepper to taste

MIX IT UP

PREHEAT OVEN TO 400 DEGREES. LIGHTLY GREASE A 9x13" BAKING DISH.

➥ Heat oil in a large skillet over medium high heat. Add mushrooms, salt, pepper and herbs. Sauté until mushrooms take on a golden color, about 5 minutes.

➥ Place a layer of white potatoes in baking dish. Cover with a thin layer of onions and mushrooms, and sprinkle with salt and pepper and small dabs of butter. Top with a layer of sweet potatoes, cover with onions and mushrooms and repeat.

➥ Pour milk over top. Add a pinch of nutmeg. Cover with foil or a tightly fitting lid.

➥ Bake 45 minutes. Remove cover and bake an additional 20 minutes until potatoes begin to brown. Let rest 5 minutes before cutting into squares.

Serves 4–6

RISOTTO CAKES

True to form, Italians almost always make more risotto than gets eaten. These golden cakes are a great way to used risotto leftovers. You can serve them as a side dish with fish, meat or grilled tofu or by themselves on a bed of fresh greens.

MIX IT UP

◈ Add Parmesan cheese to the risotto.

◈ Divide risotto in 8 equal portions and shape into patties.

◈ Press polenta or cornmeal into the surface.

◈ Heat olive oil in a large skillet over medium high heat, and add cakes. Cook on first side until golden brown, about 7 minutes. Press down with a spatula to flatten, and turn over to the other side. Cook an additional 5 minutes or until golden brown and crisp. Serve warm.

Makes 8 cakes

Ingredients

2 cups risotto, cooked, any variation

¼ cup Parmesan cheese, grated

⅓ cup polenta or fine cornmeal

2–4 TBL olive oil for frying

Tortino ai Pinoli e Verdure

ROASTED VEGETABLE PINE NUT TART

A delicious gluten-free pie crust goes a long way to reintroducing many favorites back into your diet. I use this pie crust to make savory dishes such as pot pies, quiches and vegetable tarts like this one. This roasted pepper and pine nut tart is gluten-free, dairy-free and delicious. What more could you ask for?

Ingredients: Pie crust

1 cup Mary's Baking Mix

2 TBL tapioca flour

¼ tsp salt

6 TBL butter, ghee or butter alternative, well chilled and chopped

1 egg

1 TBL or more ice water

MIX IT UP: PIE CRUST

PREHEAT OVEN TO 375 DEGREES. LIGHTLY GREASE A 9" GLASS PIE DISH OR 10" REMOVABLE-BOTTOM TART PAN.

❧ In a food processor, mix flours and salt. Pulse to blend.

❧ Cut in butter just until mixture resemble coarse meal.

❧ Add egg and water; mix just until dough forms a ball.

❧ Flatten dough into a 6" disk, and place between 2 sheets of dusted parchment or wax paper. Refrigerate 30–60 minutes.

❧ Remove dough from refrigerator and roll out between parchment paper to about an 11" round. Place in pie plate, crimp border. Refrigerate until ready to use.

continued

MIX IT UP: ROASTED VEGETABLE FILLING

PREHEAT OVEN TO 400 DEGREES. LINE A BAKING
SHEET WITH PARCHMENT PAPER OR LIGHTLY GREASE.

🍃 Remove stems and seeds from the peppers, and cut
in half. Brush the pepper on both sides with olive oil,
and sprinkle with salt and pepper. Lay skin side down
on baking sheet.

🍃 Remove skin from garlic cloves, and wrap them in
an aluminum foil pouch with 1 TBL olive oil added.
Place on the baking sheet.

🍃 In a small bowl, combine tomatoes, 1 TBL of the
olive oil, thyme, marjoram, salt and pepper. Place on
baking sheet, and bake 15 minutes.

🍃 Turn peppers and garlic pouch over, and brush the
exposed sides of the peppers with additional olive oil,
salt and pepper. Bake for an additional 15 minutes or
until peppers are tender.

🍃 Toast pine nuts, about 2–3 minutes, in a dry frying
pan, turning once or until nuts are a light brown and are
aromatic.

🍃 Transfer peppers and garlic to a cutting board, and
slice the peppers into ¼" wedges. Chop roasted garlic.

🍃 In a large bowl, combine peppers, tomatoes, garlic,
pine nuts and herbs.

🍃 Add to prepared crust. Bake 20 minutes or until
crust is a golden brown.

Makes a 9–10" tart

*Ingredients: Roasted vegetable
filling*

2 red peppers

1 orange pepper

1 yellow pepper

6 cloves garlic, roasted and chopped

2 TBL olive oil, divided

3 fresh plum tomatoes, diced

1 TBL fresh thyme, chopped

2 TBL fresh marjoram, chopped

salt and pepper to taste

olive oil for basting

½ cup pine nuts, toasted

SWEET POTATO TORTE

I am always looking for a new recipe for this traditional holiday side dish. This one combines a lovely sweet potato filling with a perfect gluten-free pie crust. Its hardy consistency will allow you to cut it into neat slices. It rivals any stuffing or side dish for the star of Thanksgiving or autumn meal.

Ingredients

Add to one Flaky Pie Crust (see page 181)

2½ lbs. sweet potatoes or garnet yams (about 3 medium-size potatoes)

1¾ cups sweetened condensed milk (1-14 oz. can)

6 TBL butter, melted

2 eggs

¼ cup pure maple syrup

1 tsp nutmeg

½ tsp cinnamon

1½ tsp salt

¾ tsp vanilla extract

DAIRY-FREE

Add 1¾ cup soy, almond or milk alternative and ¼ cup honey. If using soy creamer, eliminate the honey altogether since it is already sweetened. Substitute ghee or butter alternative for butter, both in the crust and filling.

MIX IT UP

PREHEAT OVEN TO 375 DEGREES. LIGHTLY GREASE A 9″ OR LARGER SPRINGFORM PAN.

🍃 Bake sweet potatoes until tender or easily pieced by a fork. Cut in half lengthwise, and scrape potatoes into a large bowl.

🍃 With hand mixer or food processor, beat potatoes until smooth.

🍃 Add all remaining ingredients to potatoes, and blend until ingredients are well combined.

🍃 Roll out dough to fit the springform pan, pressing the dough over the bottom and up the sides about 1–1 ½″. Make sure there are no cracks in the dough to avoid leakage.

🍃 Add filling to crust, and bake until center is set and sides begins to brown, about 1–1¼ hours.

🍃 Cool before cutting. Serve at room temperature.

Serves 12

Peperoni Arrostiti con Pinoli e Capperi

ROASTED PEPPERS WITH PINES NUTS AND CAPERS

This family recipe is so good and simple to prepare that adding it was a must. Although baked in the oven, these peppers taste as if they were roasted and peeled by hand. You can add a mixture of yellow, orange and red if you want to create a tri-colored dish. I leave out green peppers since they tend to be more acidic.

MIX IT UP

PREHEAT OVEN TO 375 DEGREES. SET OUT A LARGE GLASS BAKING DISH.

Mix all ingredients in a large bowl. Add to the baking dish.

Bake 40 minutes, uncovered, stirring mixture occasionally to keep peppers coated with oil. This dish is done when peppers are tender and can easily be pierced with a fork.

Remove from oven and cool. Serve at room temperature with *Parmesan Cheese Chips* (see page 78), rice crackers or homemade gluten-free bread.

Serves 8–10

Ingredients

4 large red peppers, corded and thinly sliced

½ cup pine nuts

¼ cup capers

2 cloves garlic, minced

¼ cup olive oil

½ cup Parmesan cheese, grated

1 tsp salt

pepper to taste

DAIRY-FREE

Substitute gluten-free bread crumbs for Parmesan cheese, and increase salt to taste.

Pomodori Ripieni

STUFFED TOMATOES WITH BASIL RICE

Although I call this a side dish, I was once served this as an antipasto in cafe in Rome. This is a great dish to make during the summer months when the tomatoes are ripe and plentiful.

Ingredients

1 TBL olive oil

½ cup sweet yellow onion, minced

2 cloves garlic, minced

¾ cup white or brown medium-grain rice

pinch of salt, plus more to taste

1½ cups water

6 large ripe tomatoes

¼ cup fresh basil, finely chopped

2 TBL fresh marjoram, finely chopped

¼ cup Parmesan cheese, finely grated

pepper to taste

DAIRY-FREE

Omit Parmesan cheese and substitute ¼ cup toasted pine nuts or walnuts, finely chopped.

MIX IT UP

PREHEAT OVEN TO 350 DEGREES. LIGHTLY GREASE A 9x9" OR LARGER GLASS BAKING DISH.

❧ In a medium saucepan, heat olive oil over medium high heat, and add onions. Sauté for 2 minutes. Add garlic, rice and a pinch of salt. Cook until rice is translucent and coated with oil, about 2 minutes. Add water to cover rice. Lower heat, and let simmer for about 20 minutes.

❧ Remove rice from stove, draining any remaining fluids, and set aside in a medium bowl.

❧ Cut tomato tops at about ¾", retaining the tomato lids, and scoop out insides. Separate the juice and pulp from the seeds with a sieve or colander.

❧ Combine the rice, basil, marjoram, Parmesan cheese, tomato juice and pulp, salt and pepper.

❧ Stuff tomatoes with the rice mixture, placing the tomato lids on top. Bake until rice is done and tomatoes are soft to touch, about 25 minutes. Serve warm.

Serves 6

MAMA CAPONE'S SAUSAGE AND PARMESAN CHEESE STUFFING

Here's another must for the Thanksgiving holiday: gluten-free stuffing. My mother has been making this recipe for 60 years. With a little gluten-free bread-baking, it's back on the menu. In my family, it simply wouldn't be Thanksgiving without it.

MIX IT UP

🍂 Over medium heat, in a large saucepan or stockpot, add olive oil and onions. Sauté until translucent, about 5 minutes. Add celery and cook for another 5 minutes.

🍂 Remove casing from the Italian sausage and add to the pan. Brown sausage, breaking it up into small, bite-size pieces. Add sage, thyme, parsley, pine nuts, salt and pepper.

🍂 Break up gluten-free bread with hands into 1" chunks. Lightly dampen with water and squeeze out any moisture. Transfer to the pan. Cook over low heat to allow any excess moisture to dry out.

🍂 Add ham and Parmesan cheese to the pan and stir, combining with the bread mixture. Remove from stove and let cool.

🍂 Place in the refrigerator for at least 2 hours. It is best when made the day before. Remove ½ hour before stuffing your bird. Add eggs; mix until combined. Either stuff the turkey, or cook stuffing in the oven in a covered baking dish for 1 hour along with the turkey, basting periodically with turkey drippings. Remove cover and let brown for an additional hour. It's also great with roast pork, chicken and wild game.

Serves 15

Ingredients

2 TBL olive oil

1 large yellow onion, diced

1 cup celery, diced

1 lb. Italian sausage, casing removed

1 TBL fresh sage, finely chopped (or 2 tsp dried sage)

2 tsp fresh thyme, finely chopped

¼ cup fresh Italian flat-leaf parsley, chopped

¼ cup pine nuts

2 tsp salt, or more to taste

½ tsp pepper, or more to taste

2 loaves gluten-free plain, sun dried tomato or herb bread recipe (or 2 dozen gluten-free rolls)

1 cup cooked ham, diced

1 cup Parmesan cheese, grated

2 eggs

I Dolci

DESSERTS
CAKES, COOKIES, PIES, TIRAMISÙ

I Dolci

Rustic Italian desserts

*T*here is nothing more satisfying than ending a fine Italian meal with a delicious homemade dessert. Italian desserts are typically more rustic than their French counterparts, many consisting of bread-like dough sweetened with honey and jam. Others contain fruits of the season wrapped in pasta frolla, a simple shortbread crust or the traditional nut-filled cookies and cakes.

Before the 1700s, sugar was a rare commodity in Italy, reserved for the court and the wealthy. The peasant population used honey as a sweetener and fresh fruits from the harvest. With the importation of sugar from the New World came pastries lightly sweetened with this delicacy, along with the addition of eggs, cocoa and homemade liqueurs. In modern times, Italian pastries have become very sophisticated, but I still love the rustic *dolci*. Not too sweet and incredibly delicious, the dolci is as rewarding as it is simple.

As in Italy, desserts in my family came with the season. Fruit crostata graced our table when the plum trees were at their peak. Deep-dish cakes and 10 varieties of cookies decorated a special three-tiered Christmas tray. Fried pastry cookies called *wands* or *cenci* (little rags) along with *pinoli* cookies and *cannoli* were piled high on Italian wedding trays. Sweet egg breads and frosted biscotti appeared at Easter, and were as coveted as the chocolate bunnies in our baskets. Occasionally we would have dessert for no special reason, enjoying chocolate biscotti or a fresh batch of *amaretti* (almond cookies) in the afternoon with a glass of sweet dandelion wine or tea.

In this section, you will find several recipes that have been handed down from generations, along with some new ones. From the simple almond cookie to the richly layered Tuscan tiramisù, these gluten-free recipes will allow you to enjoy the elemental pleasure of the Italian *dolci*.

Mary's gluten-free baking techniques

Here are some basic tips that I have found helpful in baking gluten-free desserts. Like its bread counterparts, gluten-free batters and pastry crusts tend to be stickier than ones made with wheat flour. And although you might be tempted to simply add more baking mix to handle the batter, don't do it. Since baking is an exact science, it's best to first try the recipes as they are written. After that, feel free to experiment with different fillings, flavorings or flours.

☙ One of the most important tips that I give every student is: Make a batch of Mary's Baking Mix and Mary's Baking Mix II, and store them in airtight containers in the refrigerator to have on hand. Most of the recipes in this book are written with one of these mixes in mind, and having them ready for a simple measurement makes it easy to create these recipes — and stay on course with a gluten-free diet in general.

✎ When making pie or pastry crusts, the refrigerator is your ally. Make sure eggs, water and butter are well chilled. Once the dough is mixed, store it between two pieces of parchment or wax paper, and place it in the refrigerator to chill. If during the rolling-out process your dough becomes sticky again, place it back in the refrigerator to chill for another 15 minutes or so. If you resist adding more flour and instead use the cold temperature of the refrigerator, your dough will be flaky and tender.

✎ Parchment paper is an indispensable tool for gluten-free bakers. Not only do I use it when rolling out pastry dough, I also line baking sheets with it for baking pastries.

✎ Incorporating air into batter develops texture and helps desserts rise. In almost all of these dessert recipes, you will use a mixer for 5–7 minutes to mix either eggs and sugar or eggs and butter. This process incorporates air into batter or dough — and in the case of eggs and sugar, will create what most bakers adore, a *ribbon*. A ribbon is created by mixing (and therefore breaking down) the fat in the egg. This fat attracts air and combines with the sugar. In many cases, the almighty ribbon is the only working leavening agent.

✎ *Folding* is another technique that is important to mention. Once you develop a beautiful ribbon, it is best not to deflate the batter by over-mixing. Instead, add ingredients one at a time with a large rubber spatula. Start at the center, reach to the bottom and pull up on the side. Turn the bowl a quarter turn and repeat. When all the ingredients are blended, stop folding. Except when creating a ribbon or beating egg whites, only mix ingredients at slow speed, and mix just until incorporated. Over-mixing batters will cause your baked goods to be tougher and denser.

✎ When mixing dry ingredients, I give my baking mix a shake before measuring. This helps remix the flours and adds air. When adding more than one dry ingredient to a dessert, I add them to a mixing bowl and use the whisk to blend them. Mary's Baking Mix is very light due to the flours used and really doesn't require sifting. Then again, if you are a sifter like one of my students and have an old sifter handed down from grandma, sift away.

✎ Melting chocolate can be done in a double boiler or with a tightly fitted glass bowl nested over bubbling water. Easy, right? However, there are a few things to keep in mind: First, never get water in your melting chocolate or it will seize, turning into sawdust before your very eyes. Also, take care not to allow the boiling water reach to the bottom of the double boiler or bowl since it can scorch your chocolate. When using a microwave to melt chocolate, check and stir every 30 seconds to avoid scorching.

✎ Here is my basic formula that you can use to convert your family's favorite recipes to gluten-free: Choose recipes that contain less than 2 cups gluten flour. I start by using about ¾ cup Mary's Baking Mix or Mary's Baking Mix II to every 1 cup gluten flour, and then add ½ teaspoon xanthan gum for every 1 cup of Mary's Baking Mix. I might add an egg for elasticity, and use the above techniques including ribboning or folding to help create good texture. You can also experiment with alternative gluten-free flours such as potato starch or sweet rice flour for structure. Have fun converting and creating your own gluten-free recipes!

Amaretti

ALMOND COOKIES

In Italy, everyone has a favorite recipe for amaretti, or almond cookies. Amaretti are served with espresso, used in tiramisù, and sometimes you will find them crumbled on top of a plate of streamed or sautéed greens. This light, gluten-free version has become a family favorite.

Ingredients

1 cup hazelnut meal

1⅓ cups almond meal

⅓ cup tapioca flour

½ tsp xanthan gum

1½ cups sugar, divided

4 large egg whites

1 tsp almond extract

¼ cup slivered almonds

Chef's Notes

Although this recipe is very simple, it requires plenty of time in the refrigerator, so make the dough in the morning or the day before baking. Once baked, you can store these cookies in an airtight container for up to 2 weeks.

MIX IT UP

PREHEAT OVEN TO 350 DEGREES. LINE A BAKING SHEET WITH PARCHMENT PAPER.

❧ In a large bowl, mix dry ingredients: hazelnut and almond meals, tapioca flour, xanthan gum and 1 cup of the sugar.

❧ Separate eggs, and whisk egg whites until frothy. Fold almond extract into egg whites. Add to dry ingredients; stir until incorporated. Dough will be very sticky.

❧ Cover and refrigerate for at least 10 hours or overnight.

❧ Remove chilled dough from the refrigerator. Place the remaining ½ cup sugar onto a rimmed plate or tray. Using 2 teaspoons, form a small ball of dough and drop it onto the plate. Roll the plate around until dough ball is coated with sugar. Place dough balls on baking sheet about 2" apart. Add a slivered almond on the center of each cookie, and press gently into the dough.

❧ Bake until golden brown, about 12–14 minutes. Let cool for a few minutes on the tray, and then remove to a cooling rack.

Makes 30

Biscotti di Aranciata

ORANGE PECAN BISCOTTI

The word biscotti means "twice baked." This variation on an old family recipe is so delicious, you could bake them all day long without having any leftovers. The addition of bittersweet chocolate sends them over the top. Serve them with a scoop of orange gelato, and you'll have a incredible gourmet dessert.

MIX IT UP

PREHEAT OVEN 375 DEGREES. LIGHTLY GREASE OR LINE A BAKING SHEET WITH PARCHMENT PAPER.

❧ In a large bowl, mix dry ingredients: Mary's Baking Mix II, tapioca flour, baking powder, xanthan gum and salt. Whisk until well mixed.

❧ With the paddle attachment of a hand mixer or Kitchen Aid, cream butter until white, and then add sugar. Beat for 5–7 minutes until mixture is fluffy. Add eggs one at a time, mixing on slow speed just until incorporated. Mix in orange extract, orange zest, toasted pecans and chocolate. Add dry ingredients. Mix just enough, until ingredients combine to form a soft dough.

❧ Refrigerate dough for at least 1 hour. Dough can be refrigerated overnight.

❧ On a cutting board lightly dusted with Mary's Baking Mix II, roll dough into two 2x6" logs. Place side-by-side on the baking sheet, leaving room for dough to spread.

❧ Bake for 20–22 minutes. Let cool 10 minutes. Cut log into individual biscotti about 1" thick. Lay flat on baking sheet, and return to oven for 7–10 minutes for your "twice baked" toasting. Store leftovers in an airtight container.

Makes 2 dozen

Ingredients

1½ cups Mary's Baking Mix II

¼ cup tapioca flour

1 tsp gluten-free baking powder

1 tsp xanthan gum

pinch of salt

1 stick unsalted butter

1 cup sugar

2 large eggs at room temperature

1 tsp orange extract

1 TBL orange zest

1 cup chopped pecans, toasted

4 oz. bittersweet chocolate, chopped or chips (optional)

Chef's Notes

Biscotti will be quite doughy after the initial baking, so let them cool in order to slice and handle them. I like to cut them gently with a pastry knife or a chef's knife, using the utensil to turn them on their sides for the second toasting.

Biscotti di Cioccolato e Nocciole

CHOCOLATE HAZELNUT BISCOTTI

Biscotti are the Italian version of the English biscuit. As a child, I watched my relatives dip these hard biscuit-like cookies in their afternoon cappuccino or a shot of their favorite homemade sweet wine or liqueur. It took me to adulthood to truly appreciate this version of afternoon tea. This soft biscotti is great right out of the oven.

Ingredients

2 cups Mary's Baking Mix II

½ cup unsweetened cocoa powder

¼ cup tapioca flour

1 tsp gluten-free baking powder

1 tsp xanthan gum

pinch of salt

1 stick unsalted butter, ghee or butter alternative

1 cup light brown sugar

2 large eggs at room temperature

1 tsp hazelnut extract

½ cup chopped hazelnuts

MIX IT UP

PREHEAT OVEN 350 DEGREES. LIGHTLY GREASE OR LINE A BAKING SHEET WITH PARCHMENT PAPER.

❧ In a large bowl, mix dry ingredients: Mary's Baking Mix II, cocoa powder, tapioca flour, baking powder, xanthan gum and salt. Whisk until well mixed.

❧ With the paddle attachment of a hand mixer or Kitchen Aid, cream butter until white, and then add brown sugar. Beat for 5–7 minutes until mixture is fluffy. Add eggs one at a time, mixing on slow speed just until incorporated. Mix in hazelnut extract and chopped hazelnuts. Add dry ingredients and mix just enough, until ingredients combine to form a soft dough.

❧ Refrigerate dough for at least 1 hour. Dough can be refrigerated overnight.

❧ On a cutting board lightly dusted with Mary's Baking Mix II, roll dough into two 2x6" logs. Place side-by-side on the baking sheet, leaving room for dough to spread.

❧ Bake for 20–22 minutes. Let cool 10 minutes. Cut log into individual biscotti about 1" thick. Lay flat on the baking sheet, and return to oven for 7–10 minutes for your "twice-baked" toasting. Store leftovers in an airtight container.

Makes 2 dozen

CHOCOLATE-DIPPED COCONUT ALMOND MACAROONS

This recipe is an adaptation of my sister's famous cookies, Marcia's Mad Macaroons. They are quick to make and almost impossible to bungle. The final product is a scrumptious, rich cookie in both texture and flavor.

MIX IT UP

PREHEAT OVEN TO 350 DEGREES. LIGHTLY GREASE OR LINE A BAKING SHEET WITH PARCHMENT PAPER.

◗ In a medium bowl, mix dry ingredients: coconut, sugar, Mary's Baking Mix II and xanthan gum. Stir in egg whites, vanilla and almond extract; mix until incorporated. Dough will be sticky.

◗ Mix in slivered almonds.

◗ Roll by hand into 2" ball shapes and place on baking sheet.

◗ Bake for 20–25 minutes or until light brown.

◗ When cookies are cooling, melt chocolate chips in a double boiler over low heat or over lightly simmering water. With a pastry brush or the back of a spoon, paint half of each cooled cookie with chocolate. Let rest until chocolate hardens, about 30 minutes.

Makes 2 dozen

Ingredients

2⅔ cups sweetened, shredded coconut, firmly packed

⅔ cup sugar

¼ cup Mary's Baking Mix II

½ tsp xanthan gum

4 large egg whites, unbeaten

1 tsp vanilla extract

1 tsp almond extract

1 cup slivered almonds

8 oz. semi-sweet or bittersweet chocolate chips

Savoiardi

ITALIAN LADYFINGERS

I developed this savoiardi (ladyfinger) recipe so that I could make tiramisù. Then I discovered the many uses for these sweet and delicate cookies. You can use them in a trifle, or slice them in two and make ice-cream sandwiches. Frost them with a chocolate ganache for a fancy tea cookie.

Ingredients

3 large eggs, separated

6 TBL sugar

1 tsp vanilla extract

½ cup Mary's Baking Mix II

¼ cup potato starch

1 tsp xanthan gum

1 tsp gluten-free baking powder

2 TBL confectioner's sugar

Chef's Notes

Add 4 oz. lightly boiling heavy cream or thick milk alternative such as coconut or hazelnut milk to a small bowl of 4 oz. of bittersweet or semi-sweet chocolate. Let stand for 1 minute and then whish until smooth. Presto! You have made a chocolate ganache.

MIX IT UP

PREHEAT OVEN TO 350 DEGREES. LINE A BAKING SHEET WITH PARCHMENT PAPER.

❧ In a medium bowl, beat egg whites until they form stiff peaks, about 2 minutes. Add sugar; beat again until meringue is glossy, smooth and forms stiff peaks, about 1 minute. Do not over-beat. Meringue is ruined when it forms a hard crust that breaks.

❧ Gently beat egg yolks and vanilla. Fold into meringue with a rubber spatula or wooden spoon.

❧ In a medium bowl, whisk together dry ingredients: Mary's Baking Mix II, potato starch, xanthan gum and baking powder. Sprinkle over the meringue and fold in gently.

❧ Fill a large pastry bag (#16) with batter, and use a large plain tip. If you don't have a pastry bag, use a plastic bag with the corner cut off to a ½–¾" opening. Pipe out strips of batter 3" long. Sprinkle with confectioner's sugar.

❧ Bake 10 minutes without opening the oven door to ensure the ladyfingers rise properly. Rotate the pan, and bake 4 minutes more or until cookies are a very light brown.

❧ Remove from oven, and transfer to a cooling rack. Once cool, add them to tiramisù, serve them with butter and jam, or frost them with a chocolate ganache. If you are not using the ladyfingers right away, freeze them in a plastic bag with wax paper between each layer. Cookies can stay in the freezer up to 2 weeks. When ready to use, let them thaw outside of the bag and then toast lightly in a 375 degree oven for 5 minutes.

Makes 1 dozen

Pinoli

PINE NUT COOKIES

As a kid, one of my favorite cookies on the Italian wedding tray was the unobtrusive pinule. The soft center and almond paste texture of this cookie combined with sweet nutty taste of pine nuts melted on my tongue and made me reach for more. Give me a pinule cookie with a cup of espresso, and you might find me singing the Tarantella!

MIX IT UP

PREHEAT OVEN TO 350 DEGREES. LINE A BAKING SHEET WITH PARCHMENT PAPER OR SPRAY WITH COOKING SPRAY.

To make the nut mixture, add ground pine nuts and almond meal to a food processor, and pulse to a coarse meal consistency, about 1 minute.

Add dry ingredients: tapioca flour, xanthan gum and sugar. Pulse to mix.

Add butter; pulse to combine.

Add almond extract and lemon zest, and mix to a paste-like consistency. Set aside.

In a large non-metal bowl, whip egg whites until they form soft peaks. Fold nut mixture into egg whites, stirring only until ingredients are combined. Fold in the whole pine nuts.

Cover and refrigerate at least 2 hours.

Remove dough from refrigerator. With two teaspoons or slightly moist hands (remember that dough will be sticky), form 1" balls. Place 2" apart on the baking sheet. Bake 12–14 minutes.

Makes 2 dozen

Ingredients

½ cup pine nuts, ground into meal

1 cup almond meal

⅓ cup tapioca flour

½ tsp xanthan gum

1 cup sugar

¼ cup unsalted butter, ghee or butter alternative

1 tsp almond extract

1 tsp lemon zest

4 large egg whites

½ cup pine nuts, whole

Chef's Notes

Be careful not to over-grind your nuts, or they might turn into nut butter. Adding 1 tsp sugar will coat the nuts and ensure that doesn't happen.

Cenci Fritta

WANDS

My Aunt Carmel made platters of these light, fried pastries for all of the important family events, especially weddings. We called these cookies wands, although I'm sure that is a word in dialect. Italians might call them cenci fritta, which translates to "little fried rags." Extremely light in texture and delicious in taste, I don't think you'll care what they are called as long as you can have a plate to yourself.

Ingredients

3 large eggs

½ cup sugar

1 TBL vanilla extract

¼ cup melted butter, ghee, butter alternative or vegetable oil

½ tsp salt

2¾ cups Mary's Baking Mix II

1 tsp xanthan gum

4 cups or more oil for frying, such as canola, grape seed or coconut oil

confectioner's sugar for dusting

Chef's Notes

These lovely cookies can be made days ahead of time. They'll stay fresh for quite a while if kept in a dry place covered with wax paper. Refresh with confectioner's sugar before serving.

MIX IT UP

ADD ABOUT 2" OIL TO A LARGE DUTCH OVEN OR LARGE SKILLET.

➷ In a food processor, mix together eggs, sugar, vanilla and butter.

➷ In a small bowl, whisk together dry ingredients: salt, Mary's Baking Mix II and xanthan gum.

➷ Add dry ingredients to egg mixture. Mix in food processor until dough forms a ball.

➷ Cut dough into 12 pieces. Flatten each piece with a rolling pin into a 3x4" rectangle. Roll through a pasta machine, first through the #1 (wide) setting, and then through a thinner setting (#3 is best).

➷ Place on trays dusted with Mary's Baking Mix II, and cut with the beveled side of a ravioli/pastry cutter into ribbons about 2x4". Using the beveled side of a pastry cutter, score the middle of each strip two times lengthwise without cutting the edges.

➷ Heat oil over medium high heat in a large Dutch oven or skillet to about 350 degrees, or until a droplet of batter sizzles and puffs up immediately. Add strips of dough without overcrowding. Fry until golden brown and puffed, then turn over. These little pastries will cook fast, about 30 seconds per side. Begin turning the wands as soon as you have filled the pan. Transfer to a platter lined with paper towels.

➷ When cool and well drained, mound on a platter and dust with confectioner's sugar.

Makes many...

SWEET PASTRY CRUST

A delicious gluten-free pie crust recipe goes a long way to reintroducing many favorites back into your diet. This sweet pastry crust is the perfect companion to any fruit or sweet pie filling. The best thing about it is that it's light, flaky and easy to make and handle. This one is a keeper!

MIX IT UP

PREHEAT OVEN TO 375 DEGREES. LIGHTLY GREASE A 9" GLASS PIE PLATE.

☞ In a food processor, mix dry ingredients: Mary's Baking Mix, sweet rice flour, brown sugar and salt. Pulse to blend.

☞ Cut in butter just until mixture resembles coarse meal. Add egg and water, and mix just until dough forms a ball.

☞ Flatten dough into a 6" disk, and place between two sheets of dusted parchment or wax paper. Refrigerate for ½–1 hour.

☞ Remove from refrigerator, and roll out dough between the parchment paper sheets to an 11" round. Place in pie plate, crimp border, add filling and bake according to pie or tart recipe.

Makes one 9" pie crust

Ingredients

1 cup Mary's Baking Mix

2 TBL sweet rice flour or tapioca flour

3 TBL brown sugar

¼ tsp salt

6 TBL unsalted butter, ghee or butter alternative, well chilled

1 large egg

1 TBL or more ice water

Savory pie crust variation

Eliminate brown sugar, and increase salt to ½ tsp

Chef's Notes

To make two crusts, follow the above recipe, and double it exactly. Divide dough in half, leaving one piece slightly larger than the other. Flatten each piece into a 6" disk, and place each piece between two sheets of dusted parchment or wax paper. Refrigerate for 1/2–1 hour. Remove and roll the larger dough disk between paper to fit the bottom of a 9" pie plate, about 11". Roll the second disk to about 10". Transfer bottom pastry crust to pie plate, allowing for a 1" overhang. Add filling and transfer second layer of dough to the top. Fold bottom pastry edge over the top, and crimp to seal.

SWEET PASTRY CRUST II

This pastry crust is a little sweeter and a bit more tender than the original due to the confectioner's sugar. I like to use this one when making a fruit tart.

Ingredients

1 cup Mary's Baking Mix

2 TBL sweet rice flour

4 TBL confectioner's sugar

¼ tsp salt

6 TBL unsalted butter, ghee or butter alternative, well-chilled

1 large egg

1 TBL (or more if needed) ice water

Chef's Notes

This dough will be a bit stickier and harder to handle. When you are rolling it out, if it becomes too soft, return it to the refrigerator, and cool it down until it is ready to release from the parchment paper.

MIX IT UP

LIGHTLY GREASE A 9" GLASS PIE PLATE OR A 10" TART PAN WITH A REMOVEABLE BOTTOM.

❧ In a food processor, mix dry ingredients: Mary's Baking Mix, sweet rice flour, confectioner's sugar and salt. Pulse to blend.

❧ Cut in butter just until mixture resembles coarse meal.

❧ Add egg and water, and mix just until dough forms a ball.

❧ Flatten dough into a 6" disk, and place between two sheets of dusted parchment or wax paper. Refrigerate for ½–1 hour.

❧ Remove dough from refrigerator, and roll out between parchment paper sheets to an 11" round. Place in a pie plate, crimp border, add filling and bake according to pie recipe. If making a tart, press dough into a tart pan, and fold overhanging dough back over the edge to form a double-thick crust.

Makes one 9" pie crust or one 10" tart crust

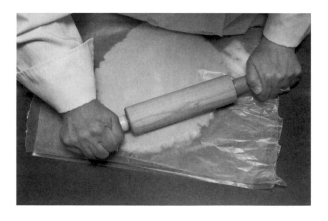

Pasta Frolla

ITALIAN SHORTBREAD CRUST

Pasta Frolla is an Italian short pastry dough that forms the basis for many jam crostatas and fruit and nut pies. This dough is a sweet flour paste comprised mostly of butter, and is very similar to shortbread. I like to use this pastry crust for a simple fruit filling such as strawberries or thinly sliced apples. You can even make a pasta frolla thumbprint cookie with a jam-filled center. Although definitely stickier due to the high amount of butter, pasta frolla is well worth it. This crust is a yummy part of the pastry.

MIX IT UP

PREHEAT OVEN TO 375 DEGREES. LIGHTLY GREASE A 9" GLASS PIE PLATE.

❧ In a food processor, mix dry ingredients: Mary's Baking Mix II, sweet rice flour, sugar and salt. Pulse to blend.

❧ Cut in butter just until mixture resembles a coarse meal.

❧ Add eggs and lemon extract. Mix just until dough forms a ball.

❧ Place between two sheets of dusted parchment paper or wax paper. Flatten to a 6" disk, and refrigerate for ½–1 hour.

❧ Remove dough from refrigerator and roll out between parchment paper to about an 11" circle. Place in pie plate, crimp border, add filling and bake according to pie recipe.

Makes one 9" pie crust, plus extra dough for lattice or jam thumbprint cookies

Ingredients

1¾ cups Mary's Baking Mix II

3 TBL sweet rice flour or tapioca flour

½ cup sugar

pinch of salt

10 TBL unsalted butter, ghee or butter alternative, well-chilled

1 large egg plus 1 egg yolk

1 tsp lemon extract

Chef's Notes

Use a little Mary's Baking Mix II on the parchment paper before putting dough in the refrigerator. If dough becomes sticky, return it to the refrigerator to cool. You will end up with more dough than you will need for a 9" pie plate. Use as a lattice top or make jam thumbprint cookies by rolling dough in a 2" ball and pressing the center down with your thumb. Add 1 tsp of your favorite jam. Bake at 350 degrees 20–22 minutes or until cookies are light brown.

Crostata di Pere e Mandorle

ALMOND PEAR CROSTATA

The crostata is Italy's version of an elegant fruit pie, a beautiful marriage of almonds and pears. And although it may seem like a lot of steps, once you get it down, it's easy to make.

Ingredients

Add to one pie crust of your choice: Sweet Pastry Crust or Pasta Frolla (see page 181 or 183)

3 cups or more water (enough to cover pears)

1 cup sugar

juice of ½ lemon

3 firm Bosc pears, peeled (about 1½ lbs.)

¾ cup raw almond meal (coarsely ground raw almonds)

2 TBL Mary's Baking Mix

½ cup sugar

6 TBL unsalted butter, ghee or butter alternative, chopped

1 large egg

1 tsp almond extract

Chef's Notes

Create a simple raspberry syrup with a 10 oz. bag frozen raspberries, 1/3 cup water and 1/4 cup sugar. Simmer until mixture resembles jam, about 10–15 minutes. Strain seeds.

MIX IT UP

PREHEAT OVEN TO 350 DEGREES. LIGHTLY GREASE A 9" PIE PLATE OR A 10" SPRINGFORM PAN.

In a medium saucepan, boil water, sugar and lemon juice until sugar dissolves. Add peeled whole pears. Poach over medium heat until pears are tender, about 25 minutes. Set saucepan aside, and let pears cool in syrup.

Pulse almonds in food processor to form a coarse meal, about 1 minute.

Add Mary's Baking Mix and sugar; pulse to mix.

Cut in butter until mixture resembles a coarse meal.

Add egg and almond extract. Mix to a paste-like consistency, about 1 minute. Refrigerate for 2 hours.

Add almond paste to prepared pie crust, and spread evenly to about 2" from edge.

Remove pears from syrup. Halve pears, removing stems, and core with a teaspoon. Cut into ½" slices. Arrange in a pattern or spread evenly over paste. Gently fold pastry crust up and over the edge of the filling, pleating it as you go. You will end up with about a 10" crostata.

Using bottom parchment paper, lift and add the crostata to a pie plate or springform pan.

Bake 45–55 minutes or until crust is golden brown and center is set. Serve at room temperature.

Serves 8–10

Crostata d' Albicocche

APRICOT CROSTATA

Here's another version of the Italian crostata. This one incorporates a rich cheese filling, and much like a cheese danish, uses an apricot jam as a topping. It is as easy as it is delicious.

MIX IT UP

PREHEAT OVEN TO 350 DEGREES. LIGHTLY GREASE A 9" PIE PLATE OR A 10" SPRINGFORM PAN.

❧ Prepare one pie crust of your choice. Place between two sheets of dusted parchment paper or wax paper, and flatten to about a 6" disk. Refrigerate for ½–1 hour.

❧ In a food processor or in a bowl, mix mascarpone cheese, egg yolk and extract. Pulse or mix until blended and creamy.

❧ Remove dough from refrigerator, and roll out between parchment paper to an 11" circle.

❧ Spread cream cheese mixture evenly on pie crust to about 2" from edge.

❧ Warm jam in a small saucepan until it is melted. Spread over the top of the cream cheese layer. Gently fold pastry crust up and over the edge of the filling, pleating it as you go. You will end up with about an 8" crostata. Sprinkle slivered almonds evenly over the top. Brush crust with an egg wash.

❧ Bake 35–40 minutes until crust is a golden brown and center is set.

❧ Serve warm or at room temperature.

Serves 8

Ingredients

Add to one pie crust of your choice: Sweet Pastry Crust or Pasta Frolla (see page 181 or 183)

4 oz. mascarpone cheese or cream cheese

1 large egg yolk

1 tsp almond extract

½ cup apricot jam

3 TBL slivered almonds

1 egg beaten plus one TBL water for egg wash (optional)

DAIRY-FREE

Substitute soy or rice cream cheese for the dairy cheese portion, and prepare a dairy-free variation of the pie crust.

Crostata di Marmellata

JAM CROSTATA

The crostata di marmellata or jam tart, is a traditional pastry found everywhere in Italy. Much like an American fruit pie, we'll finish this one with a lattice crust.

Ingredients: Lattice pie crust

1½ cups Mary's Baking Mix

3 TBL sweet rice flour or tapioca flour

⅓ cup confectioner's sugar

½ tsp salt

9 TBL unsalted butter, ghee or butter alternative, well-chilled

1 large egg

2–3 TBL ice-chilled water

Ingredients: Jam filling

2 cups good quality fruit jam such as raspberry, strawberry, blackberry, currant, pear or plum

1–2 TBL fresh lemon juice

1–2 TBL water

MIX IT UP: LATTICE PIE CRUST

❧ In a food processor, mix Mary's Baking Mix, sweet rice flour, confectioner's sugar and salt. Pulse to blend.

❧ Cut in butter until mixture resembles a coarse meal. Add egg and water. Pulse just until mixture forms a soft ball.

❧ Place between two sheets of dusted parchment paper or wax paper, and flatten to about a 6″ disk.

❧ Refrigerate for ½–1 hour. Roll chilled dough between the parchment paper sheets to a 12–14″ disk.

❧ Peel off one layer of parchment paper, and flip dough over onto pie plate. Peel back second layer of parchment paper; trim excess dough off edge. Refrigerate pie plate with rolled out crust until filling is ready. Wrap extra dough in lightly dusted parchment paper, and place in the refrigerator.

MIX IT UP: JAM FILLING

PREHEAT OVEN TO 350 DEGREES. LIGHTLY GREASE A 9″ DEEP-DISH PIE PLATE.

❧ In a small saucepan, heat jam, water and lemon juice to taste. Start with 1 TBL at a time, and add more to taste.

❧ Spoon jam filling into prepared crust. Prepare lattice top, and place on the pie (see page 181 for double crust).

❧ Bake 20 minutes, just until dough begins to brown. Be careful not to overcook this crostata, or it may result in a very hard crust and a sticky jam center. Remove and let cool before serving.

Serves 8

Crostata di Limone

LEMON CURD TART

This delightful light lemon tart starts with a simple lemon curd. Light and creamy, yet full of fresh flavor, this dessert is the Italian version of the French lemon mousse pie. It can be served plain, or dressed up with whipped cream. I like the dairy-free version just as much.

MIX IT UP

PREHEAT OVEN TO 375 DEGREES. LIGHTLY GREASE A 10" TART PAN WITH REMOVEABLE BOTTOM.

✎ Zest and juice lemons. Set aside 1 TBL lemon zest for the top.

✎ Beat egg yolks and sugar together just until mixed. Add lemon juice and zest, and whisk together. Add butter in chunks.

✎ Transfer mixture to a double boiler. Stir over gently boiling water until mixture thickens, about 5–7 minutes. Do not let mixture boil, or you will cook your eggs. Remove from heat. Cool in a glass bowl.

✎ Remove pastry dough from refrigerator and roll out between the parchment paper to an 11" circle. Press dough into tart pan, folding overhanging dough back over the edge to form a double-thick crust. Cover the bottom with parchment paper, and add pie weights or 2 cups of dried beans to prevent the crust from collapsing. Bake 25–30 minutes, until crust is a golden brown. Remove weights after 15 minutes.

✎ In a clean, dry bowl, whip egg whites until they form soft peaks. Whip cream and vanilla until it resembles whipped cream.

✎ Fold egg whites and cream mixture into cooled lemon curd.

✎ Spread filling into prepared tart shell. Cool in refrigerator for 1–2 hours. Sprinkle with lemon zest, and decorate with extra whipped cream. Can be refrigerated overnight.

Serves 8–10

Ingredients

Add to one pie crust of your choice: Sweet Pastry Crust or Pasta Frolla (see page 181 or 183)

2 lemons, zested and juiced

4 large eggs, (separated)

½ cup sugar

3 TBL unsalted butter

¼ cup heavy cream, light cream or milk

1 tsp vanilla extract

DAIRY-FREE

Substitute ¼ cup milk alternative or coconut milk. For cream, substitute 1 tsp vanilla. Without whipping, fold directly into cooled lemon curd. Fold in egg whites.

Chef's Notes

Coconut milk is a wonderful substitute for heavy cream. High in good saturated fats, it has a thick and creamy texture.

MAYA'S CARAMEL APPLE CROSTATA

My daughters and I catered a friend's wedding that featured a dessert-only reception. We filled three banquet tables full of scrumptious desserts. This caramel apple crostata, my daughter Maya's invention, stole the show.

Ingredients

Add to one pie crust of your choice: Sweet Pastry Crust or Pasta Frolla (see page 181 or 183)

1 cup dark brown sugar

½ cup water

¾ cup heavy cream

5 TBL unsalted butter, chopped and divided

4–5 firm apples such as Granny Smith or McIntosh (about 1½ lbs.)

2 tsp lemon peel, grated

DAIRY-FREE

Substitute ghee or butter alternative for butter. Use milk alternative such as soy, almond or coconut milk instead of heavy cream.

Chef's Notes

If your caramel mixture begins to harden, reheat briefly, stirring until you have a workable consistency. It will melt completely while baking.

MIX IT UP

PREHEAT OVEN TO 375 DEGREES. LIGHTLY GREASE OR LINE WITH PARCHMENT PAPER A 10" SPRINGFORM PAN.

❧ Prepare one pie crust of your choice. Place dough between two sheets of dusted parchment or wax paper, and flatten to a 6" disk. Refrigerate for ½–1 hour.

❧ Combine brown sugar with water in a small saucepan. Bring to a boil. Without stirring, boil syrup until it becomes a golden brown, swirling the pan to combine and brushing down sides with a wet pastry brush.

❧ Stir in cream and 3 TBL of the butter until mixture is smooth; set aside.

❧ Remove dough from refrigerator, and roll out between the parchment paper to an 11" circle. Place back in refrigerator until ready to use.

❧ Slice apples into ½" wedges. Arrange apple wedges in a concentric circle pattern on the prepared pie crust. Sprinkle with lemon peel, and dot with the remaining 2 TBL butter.

❧ Add the caramel syrup over the top.

❧ Gently fold pastry crust up and over the edge of the filling, pleating it as you go. You will end up with about an 8" crostata.

❧ Bake 35–40 minutes, or until pastry is a golden brown and apples can be pierced easily with a fork.

Serves 8

JO'S CHOCOLATE RICOTTA PIE

I made this delicious gluten-free pie for my Italian friend's birthday. It brought tears to her eyes, filling her with culinary memories from her childhood. The light yet rich chocolate ricotta filling is wrapped in a sweet pastry crust, creating a sensational pastry. For this recipe, we'll use the Double Crust Recipe.

MIX IT UP

PREHEAT OVEN TO 350 DEGREES. LIGHTLY GREASE A 9" PIE PLATE.

✏ Prepare Sweet Pastry Crust: Double Crust Recipe. Divide into two parts, one slightly larger for the bottom of the pie. Place each dough piece between two sheets of dusted parchment paper or wax paper. Flatten to two 6" disks, and refrigerate for ½–1 hour.

✏ In a small bowl, beat egg yolks and sugar together.

✏ In a double boiler, combine egg mixture, Mary's Baking Mix and cream. Cook over simmering water until the mixture begins to thicken.

✏ In another double boiler or in the microwave, melt chocolate chips for about 1 minute.

✏ Stir chocolate into egg mixture, and add hazelnut extract. Let cool.

✏ Stir ricotta cheese, cinnamon and lemon zest into cooled egg mixture. Let rest for 15 minutes.

✏ Remove pie crust from refrigerator. Roll the larger dough disk between parchment or wax paper to fit the bottom of a 9" pie plate (about 11"). Place in pie plate, and crimp border.

✏ Roll out second disk to about 10". Set aside.

✏ Add filling. Transfer second layer of dough to the top. Fold top edge of dough under the bottom, and crimp to seal.

✏ Bake 35–40 minutes until the crust is golden brown. Serve cool, garnished with a dusting of confectioner's sugar, shaved chocolate or whipped cream.

Serves 8

Ingredients

Add to Sweet Pastry Crust: Double Crust Recipe (see page 181)

3 large egg yolks

⅓ cup sugar

2 TBL Mary's Baking Mix

1 cup light cream or milk

½ cup semisweet chocolate chips

2 tsp hazelnut extract

1 cup gluten-free ricotta cheese, well-drained

½ tsp cinnamon

1 TBL lemon zest

DAIRY-FREE

Substitute 1 cup firm tofu blended with 1 TBL milk alternative for ricotta cheese. Substitute soy creamer, coconut milk, soy milk, almond milk or milk alternative for light cream.

CARAMELIZED ITALIAN PLUM CAKE

A version of the pineapple upside-down cake, the caramelized plum tartin is a rewardingly rich and elegant dessert. The tart taste of dark purple Italian plums are my favorite for this recipe, although you might use other fruits such as Bosc pears or Granny Smith apples. The sponge cake is moist and tender and is a great white cake all by itself.

Ingredients

1¾ cups sugar (divided)

⅓ cup water

2 lbs. Italian plums (or dark purple or red plums), pitted and sliced into wedges

6 TBL unsalted butter

2 large eggs

⅓ cup plain yogurt

½ tsp lemon zest

1 tsp vanilla extract

¾ cup Mary's Baking Mix II

2 tsp xanthan gum

½ tsp gluten-free baking powder

pinch of salt

DAIRY-FREE

Substitute ghee or butter alternative, and use plain flavored soy or rice yogurt. Coconut milk is another great substitution for yogurt.

MIX IT UP

PREHEAT OVEN TO 350 DEGREES. GENEROUSLY GREASE A 9" GLASS PIE PLATE.

❧ To make the simple syrup, combine 1 cup of the sugar with the water in small saucepan, and bring to a boil. Without stirring, boil syrup until it becomes a deep amber, swirling the pan to combine and brushing down sides with wet pastry brush, about 10–15 minutes.

❧ Arrange plums in a spiral pattern on bottom of pie plate, and pour the simple syrup evenly over the plums.

❧ In a food processor or with a hand mixer, beat butter until white. Add the remaining ¾ cup sugar, and beat together 3–5 minutes.

❧ At slow speed, add wet ingredients: first add eggs one at a time, then add yogurt, lemon zest and vanilla. Mix until combined.

❧ In a small bowl, whisk together dry ingredients: Mary's Baking Mix II, xanthan gum, baking powder and salt. Add to batter, and mix at low speed just until combined.

❧ Pour cake batter over the plums, and bake for 35–40 minutes or until cake tester comes out clean.

❧ Let cool completely. Using a flat plate, invert the cake onto the plate. The caramelized fruit topping will release slowly. If any fruit sticks after inversion, remove and add back to the top in its defined spot by hand. Serve dusted with confectioner's sugar.

Serves 8

Dolce di Natale

CHRISTMAS CAKE

I call this luscious chocolate soufflé cake "Christmas Cake," although it is a wonderful dessert anytime of the year. It is especially nice at holiday time when there are large gatherings and the dessert needs to go a long way. The moist, rich center is complemented by the crusty chocolate outside. I like to decorate this with a sprinkle of confectioner's sugar and rim it with fresh raspberries, strawberries or a toasted almond brittle. Slice this cake thinly, and it will serve a kingdom... or your extended family.

MIX IT UP

PREHEAT OVEN TO 325 DEGREE. LIGHTLY GREASE A 10" SPRINGFORM PAN.

❧ In a double boiler, melt chocolate. Remove from heat. Let cool about 10 minutes.

❧ In a small saucepan, melt butter. Remove from heat. Let cool about 10 minutes.

❧ Separate eggs; place whites into a large bowl and yolks into a Kitchen Aid or a large hand mixer bowl. Beat egg yolks until a light yellow, about 1 minute. Add sugar, and beat until you create a heavy ribbon, about 5–7 minutes.

❧ Add vanilla and hazelnut extracts. Mix on slow speed just until incorporated.

❧ Add melted chocolate and butter, and fold in with a large spoon or rubber spatula until blended (see *Folding*, page 173).

❧ In another bowl, shift together dry ingredients: Mary's Baking Mix II, xanthan gum, cocoa and salt. Sprinkle on top of the batter, and fold in gently.

❧ Whip the egg whites to soft peaks, and fold into batter just until all egg whites are mixed.

❧ Pour batter into springform pan. Bake for 1 hour and 15 minutes. Cake will rise like a soufflé and fall when it cools. Let cool completely. Sprinkle with confectioner's sugar, and decorate with sliced strawberries or whole raspberries.

Serves 24

Ingredients

12 oz. bittersweet chocolate

3½ sticks unsalted butter, or 28 TBL ghee or butter alternative

12 large eggs, separated

2 cups sugar

2 tsp vanilla extract

½ TBL hazelnut extract

¼ cup Mary's Baking Mix II

1 tsp xanthan gum

½ cup unsweetened cocoa

½ tsp salt

Chef's Notes

A traditional soufflé is served piping hot directly from the oven. This cake, however, is better after it sits and literally collapses in on itself, creating a uneven, crusty top and a soft delicate center. To achieve this, just let it cool — it will happen all by itself.

CHOCOLATE MINT SOFT-CENTER CAKES

The first time I tasted this pudding cake, I was hooked. Not quite flourless and not quite a chocolate mousse, it has a little bit of both. A quick dessert — you can whip it up in a pinch — this scrumptious cake makes a dinner party dessert easy.

Ingredients

6 oz. bittersweet or semisweet chocolate, chopped

1 stick unsalted butter, chopped, or 8 TBL ghee or butter alternative

3 large eggs plus 3 large egg yolks

⅓ cup sugar

¼ cup Mary's Baking Mix

1 ¼ tsp peppermint extract

¼ tsp salt

Chef's Notes

Do not overcook, or you will lose the soft center. Remove when center is slightly concave and looks moist. To promote even baking when using muffin tins, fill empty muffin cups 3/4 full with water.

MIX IT UP

PREHEAT OVEN TO 375 DEGREES. LIGHTLY GREASE 6 RAMEKINS OR CUSTARD CUPS, OR A 12-CUP MUFFIN TIN.

🍃 In a small saucepan, combine chocolate and butter. Stir until melted and smooth. Set aside to cool.

🍃 In a large mixing bowl with a hand mixer or a Kitchen Aid, beat eggs and sugar until they form a thick, pale ribbon, about 5–7 minutes.

🍃 Add Mary's Baking Mix and blend.

🍃 Add chocolate mixture, peppermint extract and salt. Mix until incorporated.

🍃 Divide equally between ramekins, custard cups or muffin tins. This batter will fill 8 spaces of the muffin tin.

🍃 Place ramekins or custard cups on baking sheet. Bake only until sides are set and middle is slightly loose and glossy, about 8–10 minutes. If using a muffin tin, check for doneness at about 6–8 minutes.

🍃 Remove cakes from oven, and loosen sides with a knife. Invert onto a dessert plate and let cool. Sprinkle with confectioner's sugar or sweetened cocoa. Garnish with a fresh mint leaf if desired.

Makes 6–8 individual cakes

Torta di Pinoli

PINE NUT TORTE

Although only slightly sweet, this traditional rustic Italian cake is surprisingly rich. You might serve this with a simple raspberry sauce or vanilla ice cream, although it is great plain.

MIX IT UP

PREHEAT OVEN TO 375 DEGREES. LIGHTLY GREASE A 10" SPRINGFORM PAN.

❦ With a hand mixer or Kitchen Aid, cream butter until pale. Add sugar. Beat for 5–7 minutes until mixture is fluffy.

❦ Whisk together dry ingredients: Mary's Baking Mix II, sweet rice flour, xanthan gum and salt. Slowly add dry ingredients to the butter mixture, stirring until mixture resembles coarse meal.

❦ Whisk eggs, lemon peel and almond extract in a small bowl. Gently stir egg mixture into the butter batter.

❦ Pour into prepared pan. Arrange pine nuts on top, pressing them gently into the batter.

❦ Bake for 30 minutes or until a toothpick comes out clean. Let cool completely. Sprinkle with confectioner's sugar and serve.

Serves 8

Ingredients

10 TBL unsalted butter, ghee or butter alternative

1 cup light brown sugar

1½ cups Mary's Baking Mix II

2 TBL sweet rice flour

½ tsp xanthan gum

pinch of salt

3 large egg yolks at room temperature

1 large egg at room temperature

2 tsp lemon peel

1 tsp almond extract

½ cup pine nuts

Chef's Notes

Create a simple raspberry syrup with a 10 oz. bag frozen raspberries, 1/3 cup water and 1/4 cup sugar. Simmer until mixture resembles jam, about 10–15 minutes. Strain through a fine sieve. Or puree a thawed 10 oz. bag of frozen raspberries with syrup in a blender. Strain.

Cannoli

SOFT-SHELLED CANNOLI

One of my favorite desserts is the Italian cannoli. When I lost the ability to eat the real ones, I invented a soft-shelled, gluten-free version. Only slightly different in texture, this simple version has all of the taste of the real cannoli without the fried crust.

Ingredients

Add to one recipe Marie's Crepes (see page 62)

10 oz. gluten-free ricotta cheese

1 cup super-fine granulated sugar

2 oz. miniature semisweet chocolate chips

4 TBL pistachio nuts, minced (divided)

MIX IT UP

In a small bowl, combine ricotta cheese, sugar, chocolate chips and 2 tablespoons of the pistachio nuts. Refrigerate for 1 hour.

Prepare one recipe Marie's Crepes.

Add ¼ cup of filling to each crepe, and roll into a cylinder shape. Sprinkle ends with remaining pistachio nuts. Refrigerate until you are ready to serve.

Garnish with a Chocolate Ganache (see page 178) or Raspberry Sauce (see page 193), and serve.

Makes 8 servings

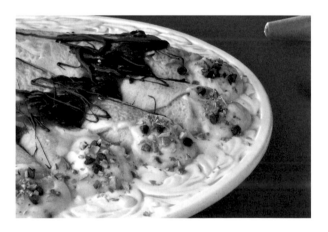

Tiramisù

TUSCAN TIRAMISÙ

This is a rich dish, but for tiramisù lovers, it's a dream come true and well worth the effort. The ladyfingers, or savoiardi, in this recipe are delightfully light and add just the right amount of sponge to soak up the rich zabaglione, brandy and espresso sauce. Literally translated, tiramisù means "pick me up," and is the Italian answer to the English trifle.

MIX IT UP

LINE A LOAF PAN OR SQUARE BAKING DISH WITH PARCHMENT PAPER.

✎ In a medium bowl, mix together espresso, sugar and brandy. Reserve ¼ cup for soaking ladyfingers.

✎ Mix together egg yolk and mascarpone cheese. Add espresso to mascarpone and stir until smooth.

✎ Soak ladyfingers one at a time in the reserved brandy coffee mixture. Do not over-soak. Place in the baking dish, covering bottom completely.

✎ Spread ⅓ of the cream cheese mixture and ⅓ of the shaved chocolate over the ladyfingers. Repeat for two more layers.

✎ Refrigerate 2 hours to set. When ready to serve, top with whipped cream, the remaining shaved chocolate and a dusting of cocoa powder. This dessert can be made a day in advance.

Serves 6

Ingredients

½ cup espresso or double-strong coffee

½ cup sugar

¼ cup brandy

1 large egg yolk

8 oz. mascarpone cheese, Italian cream cheese or cream cheese

12 Ladyfinger Cookies (see page 178)

4 oz. semisweet chocolate, shaved cocoa powder for dusting

whipped cream for topping

DAIRY-FREE

Substitute tofu cream cheese for mascarpone cheese, and use soy whipped cream for the topping.

Gelato All' Arancia

ORANGE GELATO

This Italian gelato or sorbet goes exceptionally well with biscotti or served alone as a refreshing dessert. It can be made in an ice cream maker or frozen in a shallow glass baking dish. Try lemon or lime as an alternate flavor for this delicious treat.

Ingredients

1½ cups sugar

2 cups water

1½ cups fresh-squeezed orange juice (from about 4 oranges)

1 TBL orange zest, finely grated

MIX IT UP

SET OUT A 9x13" GLASS BAKING DISH.

To make the simple syrup, in a medium saucepan mix sugar and water, and bring to a boil over medium high heat. Lower heat and simmer without stirring until sugar is completely dissolved, about 5–7 minutes. Set aside to cool.

In a medium bowl, combine orange juice and zest.

Mix cooled syrup into juice bowl. If you are using an ice cream maker, follow the manufacturer's instructions for sorbet, about 30 minutes. If not, pour mixture in the baking dish and put into the freezer. Stir every hour until gelato sets, not frozen hard, about 5–6 hours.

Makes eight ½-cup servings

Gelato Al Limone

LEMON GELATO

Here's another simple gelato recipe that I call lemon ice. Serve this simple dessert with fresh berries, or in between courses to clear the palate.

MIX IT UP

≫ Heat water and sugar to make syrup, about 5 minutes. Add lemon juice and lemon zest. Let cool.

≫ Freeze lemon mixture until solid.

≫ Place frozen lemon syrup and egg white in a food processor and blend. Cover and return to freezer for ½ hour or until ready to serve.

≫ If you have an ice cream maker, add to machine's bowl after the second step. Omit the egg white and freeze according to manufacturer's instructions. When finished, cover bowl and keep in the freezer until ready to serve.

Makes 2 cups

Ingredients

1 cup water

1 cup sugar

1 cup fresh-squeezed lemon juice (from about 4 lemons)

2 TBL lemon zest (from about 2 lemons)

1 large egg white

Cookies

Wands.

Ingred:
   6 eggs.
   1 tsp salt
   1 cup sugar
   1/2 cup oil
   2 tbls vanilla

Add flour until you can knead it
to be able to roll on board cut into
strips & fry in deep oil.
   Sprinkle & confectioners sugar
(# 3 or # 4 pasta machine)

Aunt Carmel's Wands Recipe

198

Gluten-Free, Who Me?

$\mathcal{L}$ike most people with celiac disease, my road to its discovery was a serpentine one. From a young age, I suffered from health conditions ranging from stomach ulcers, migraine headaches, delayed development, ulcerative colitis, and finally lymphoma. I was told by the medical community that my ailments were due to genetics and that there was nothing I could to do about it. Throughout the process, I keep asking the question, why? Why had both my paternal grandmother and grandfather suffered with Chron's and ulcerative colitis and later cancer? What were we all doing that have caused the same ill health? After 10 years of misdiagnosis and personal exploration, I began to understand my family's secret. I had inherited celiac disease from the long line of relatives before me.

Thanks to our combined voices in the celiac community, in the last few years, the gluten-free picture has become clearer in both in the medical field and in the public eye. Medical journals and websites have published close to 1 million articles on this very subject. Those of you who resist the idea that the wheat bagel you had for breakfast could have a connection with joint pain in the afternoon, read on. I think you'll find it fascinating.

What is gluten?

Gluten is a storage protein, a prolamin, that is found in wheat, rye and barley. These prolamins cause damage to people who have gluten sensitivity or celiac disease. For all practical purposes, we will put them under the umbrella of gluten grains.

What about oats? Since wheat, rye and barley are grown in the same fields as oats and are harvested with same machinery and stored in the same silos, oats are most certainly cross-contaminated. There are new gluten-free oats on the market that claim no cross-contamination. Although I haven't included them in my diet, they are reported to be safe. Still, the National Celiac Sprue Association (NCSA) does not recommend adding oats to the diet of someone newly diagnosed with celiac disease for at least the first two years. (For a more complete list of safe and forbidden grains, see page 16.)

Celiac disease and the gluten-free diet

According to The National Foundation for Celiac Awareness (NFCA), celiac disease affects one out of every 133 Americans. Ninety seven percent of people with celiac disease are undiagnosed and go untreated. That means that almost 3 million Americans have celiac disease and only about 100,000 are properly diagnosed. Furthermore, the July 2008 edition of *Gastroenterology* reported that it takes an average time of 10 years to get an accurate diagnosis of celiac disease.

Celiac disease is a digestive condition triggered by the consumption of gluten. Hair-like structures called *villi* line the small intestine. The villi's job is to increase absorption of nutrients gathered from foods as they pass through the small intestine. Repeated consumption of gluten results in the blunting and shortening of the villi. In extreme cases, the villi are flattened. A condition of malabsorption can develop when flattened villi can no longer able to absorb the vitamins and minerals from food taken in.

The tip of the villi produces the enzyme lactase that breaks down the sugar lactose. When the villi become blunted, many people with celiac disease lose their ability to digest lactose. When the villi returns to full health, many people are able to digest lactose again.

Even trace amounts of gluten in the diet can be damaging, whether or not it causes signs or symptoms. People with any stage of gluten sensitivity have an immune system that sees gluten as toxic, a foreign invader, and attacks it. Gluten sensitivity, gluten intolerance or celiac disease can take the form of "silent celiac disease," which can erode at people's general health damaging the intestinal lining of the gut. Some people with celiac and gluten sensitivity exhibit gastrointestinal symptoms after ingesting gluten including: gas, bloating, constipation or diarrhea, heartburn, acid reflux and nausea.

The majority of people, however, have what is called extra intestinal symptoms, which occur outside the digestive tract. Here a few lesser known symptoms: ADD/ADHD, fatigue, delayed growth or failure to thrive, inability to concentrate, infertility, depression, hair loss, night blindness, low blood sugar (hypoglycemia), rosacea, lupus, canker sores, seizure, headaches (including migraines), weight gain and weight loss, joint, bone, or muscle pain, respiratory problems, nosebleeds, general swelling and inflammation, eczema/psoriasis, acne, muscle cramping and vitamin and mineral deficiencies. (*Living Gluten-Free for Dummies* by Korn, Wiley Publishing, 2006.)

How serious is this condition? Many physicians and scientists now believe celiac disease is the underlying cause of many other health problems ranging from chronic fatigue, autoimmune diseases, osteoporosis, type 1 diabetes, infertility, heart disease and even some cancers. For more information, here are a few websites that have been recommended by the NCSA: celiaccentral.org, csaceliacs.org, celiac.nih.gov/Default.aspxbidmc, harvard.edu, and celiac.com.

The good news is that as soon as people with gluten-sensitivities stop eating gluten, their villi will begin to heal. They are tenacious little fibers and they want to grow back. Over time and with a careful gluten diet, health can be fully restored.

Autism and a gluten-free, casein-free diet

There has been significant research (and more on the way) that shows that some people with autism exhibit remarkable behavior improvement on a gluten-free, casein-free diet. Although it may be the same allergy as people with celiac disease, it is a different mechanism at work. People with autism may actually metabolize casein and gluten into a form of an opiate similar to heroin. When eating either casein or gluten, they get high and become addicted to it. This may account for many of the traits typical of autistic children: finger flicking, monotonous body movement, spinning, head banging. The prevalence of celiac disease is higher in autistic people than in the general public.

Metric Conversions

U.S.	METRIC
1/4 teaspoon	1.25 ml
1/2 teaspoon	2.5 ml
1 teaspoon	5 ml
1 Tablespoon	15 ml
1/4 cup	60 ml
1/3 cup	80 ml
1/2 cup	120 ml
2/3 cup	160 ml
3/4 cup	180 ml
1 cup	240 ml
1 pint	480 ml
1 quart	960 ml
1 gallon	3.84 liters
1 ounce	28 grams
2 ounces	56 grams
4 ounces (1/4 pound)	112 grams
8 ounces (1/2 pound)	227 grams
16 ounces (1 pound)	454 grams
2.2 pounds	1 kilogram

Oven Temperatures

FAHRENHEIT	CELSIUS
275	140
300	150
325	160
350	180
375	190
400	200
425	220
450	230
475	240
500	260

Index

Suppliers

Authentic Foods
1850 W. 169th Street, Suite B
Gardena, CA 90247
800-806-4737, www.authenticfoods.com
Tapioca starch, potato starch and gluten-free flours

Bella Gluten-Free
PO Box 355
Niwot, CO 80544
303-999-0225, www.bellaglutenfree.com
Designed by Author Mary Capone, Bella Gluten-Free offers 100% natural allergen-free baking mixes including an All Purpose Mix that can be substituted for Mary's Baking Mix.

Bob's Red Mill Natural Foods
5209 SE International Way
Milwaukie, OR 97222
503-654-3215, www.bobsredmill.com
Stone ground gluten-free flours and other baking supplies

Information and Resources

Autism Society of America
4340 East-West Hwy., Suite 350
Bethesda, Maryland 20814
800-328-8476, www.autism-society.org

National Celiac Sprue Association
PO Box 31700
Omaha, NE 68131-0700
877-272-4272, www.csaceliacs.org

Living Without Magazine
PO Box 420234
Palm Coast, FL 32142-0234
800-474-8614, www.livingwithout.com

Wheat-Free Gourmet
5836 Park Lane Road
Longmont, CO 80503
303-807-0050, www.wheatfreegourmet.com

*G*rowing up in an Italian household filled with restaurateurs and great cooks, Mary Capone learned the foundations of classic Italian cuisine from her family's boisterous kitchens. As a celiac, she has since reinvented this scrumptious cuisine to meet the needs of gluten-free dieters. Her articles and recipes have appeared in *The Herb Quarterly, Energy for Women, Eatingwell.com, Living Without Magazine, Livingwithout.com, Delicious Living Magazine* and *Delight Gluten-Free.* She is currently the director of *The Wheat-Free Gourmet Cooking School,* www.wheatfreegourmet.com, and has taught over 1500 students from around the world. Mary is the owner of *The Wheat-Free Gourmet* and *Bella Gluten-Free, Beautiful Food…Simply Delicious,* www.bellaglutenfree.com, featuring an allergen-free line of dry mixes. She lives in Boulder, Colorado with her loving family.